SECRET FAMILY CAVES—
REVEALED FOR THE FIRST TIME
TO ANY WESTERNER

Mazière and his wife had a close relationship
with the people of Easter Island. To them
alone did the Polynesians reveal secrets of
their lives, legends and traditions. With this
information and other explorations, the author
works to untangle the mystery of the mute
stone giants whose sightless eyes stare out to
sea from Easter Island's volcanic slopes. An
intriguing probe into the past and present of
unique Easter Island.

"MYSTERIES OF EASTER ISLAND is geography, history and sleuthing reduced to the
finest essence."

—Columbus Dispatch

MYSTERIES OF EASTER ISLAND

Francis Maziere

WITH PHOTOGRAPHS BY THE AUTHOR

A TOWER BOOK

MYSTERIES OF EASTER ISLAND

Tower Publications, Inc.
185 Madison Avenue
New York, New York 10016

Copyright © MCMLXV by Robert Laffont

Copyright © MCMLXVIII in the English translation by
Wm. Collins Sons & Co. Ltd.

Library of Congress Catalog Card Number 67-12443

Published by special arrangement with
W. W. Norton & Company, Inc.

To the people of the island
who died at sea while trying to escape

Contents

Prologue

Far, far away, where the long smoothness of the Pacific swell is torn and shattered on jutting lava crags; where the astonished winds from the Antarctic howl round unmoving giants of stone; far away, where the eight hundred survivors of a forgotten world are slowly dying in silence and the frigate birds their forefathers once ritually watched for no longer come to rest in their flight, there rises from the sea the loneliest island in the world. It is the island the inhabitants call Matakiterani—'eyes gazing at the sky'—and which the first sailors from the world of vanity baptized Easter Island.

This rocky fragment rising out of the expanse of the Pacific Ocean thrust itself up in silence and has died in oblivion. Whether it is indeed the sole surviving indication of the lost continent or archipelago of Hiva no one can ever know. We can only beg the reader to make his way forward, as painfully as though he too were advancing over the island's windswept volcanic slag, to discover with us this dark solemn world whose last faint heart-beats we detected—a world which may none the less possess a strange and unexpected relevance to our own.

For in an age when the island's night sky is crossed by spacecraft following the strange path of the magnetic equator, watched calmly by men whom we rashly style primitive because the nature of their intelligence differs so radically from our own, it is unwise to suppose that all perception, all insight belonging to those whom the islanders call 'the Others' has entirely disappeared . . .

MYSTERIES OF EASTER ISLAND

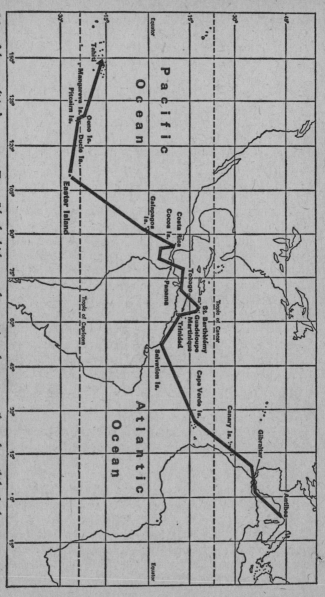

Map of the expedition's voyage to Easter Island which covered approximately 12,000 miles and entailed 160 days at sea

ONE

Towards the Navel of the World

On 22 November 1962 our boat left France for the prolonged and arduous voyage that was to teach us the changing map of the stars—the stars we watched night after night. A hundred and sixty days of sea and of living upon the sea; a hundred and sixty days of fighting against the winds, against the vastness of the ocean, and sometimes against oneself.

Our boat was a stout ketch with a Bermuda rig; she was fifty-two feet at the waterline, sixty-five feet overall, with a beam of nearly fifteen feet and a draught of seven feet ten inches. With her mizzen, mainsail, two jibs and a square sail she could carry 1,130 square feet of canvas; she had a Berliet-Diesel engine; and to carry her through to success she had four men and one woman. We had little money, but we were rich in the help of all those who had come to our assistance and whose names are to be found inscribed at the end of this book.

It had been four years of struggle before we left, and it was to be two more before our mission was accomplished. Our aim was to get to Easter Island, there to carry out our archeological investigations, and, by way of ending the expedition, to go back to Tahiti through the Gambier archipelago—a very long voyage, most of which we were to carry out under sail, in order to study the trade winds and the currents, and the possibilities

13

they provided for migrations across the Atlantic, from Africa to the mouths of the Amazon, and then across the South Pacific.

Supplies reach Easter Island, which is at present Chilean territory, only once a year, aboard a naval vessel which stays ten days or so in the Hangaroa roads. So the only way we could carry out our plan was to go to the island in our own boat, to be free to work; and that was why we had to undertake a voyage that belonged to an entirely different age.

This was how our journey ran: we sailed from Antibes for Gibraltar, the Canaries, where we wanted to see the Guanche remains, and the Cape Verde islands, which were particularly interesting to us because of the earliest voyages of the Phoenicians, who we believed might have followed the most southerly path of the trade winds towards the mouths of the Amazon. And so to Brazil, Guiana, the Lesser Antilles, Curaçao, Panama, and the Pacific coast of Costa Rica, where we carried on with our quest, especially on the slopes of the El Baru volcano where our stratigraphical research brought to light a considerable number of figurines, the evidence of a civilization distinctly Mongoloid in character. Then, sailing by way of the remarkable Cocos Island, we set our course for the Galapagos Islands. On 3 January 1963 we came in sight of the archipelago, and at nightfall we anchored in Darwin Bay. Now, after the quietness of the long crossing, we lay there in the cold night, and the barking of the sea-lions, echoing from the walls of this sunken crater, gave the darkness the weird feeling of another world. Added to this were the cries of myriads of nesting sea-birds startled by the beams of our searchlight. The Galapagos Islands, with their great crested iguanas swimming in the sea, their extraordinary birds, their sea-lions, their penguins and their whales passing by in migration, are a delightful example of a world that animals alone have managed to reconquer.

Unfortunately, we could stay only ten days in the archipelago, and although I very much wanted to make a few trial archeological digs, there was no question of carrying out any serious investigation. But we believe these islands must hold important traces of those who came from mainland America and who set off once more in pursuit of the setting sun, and that Pacific archeologists will discover them. We should have been all the more delighted to dig, I may say, for at Panama we had learned that pre-Columbian pottery had been discovered on the Galapagos.

Alas, we were obliged to weigh anchor at half past eight on the morning of 13 January, and sail from Elizabeth Bay to attempt the vast, lonely, ocean crossing towards the island we called the Navel of the World. Sadly we put back into the sea the friendly little penguins who had been living aboard. Sadly we watched the disappearance of that fiery archipelago whose creatures dwell in the ultimate happiness of freedom.

The great Humboldt current that governs the strange life of those islands now ran directly across our path; the sea was very cold, and we often met whales. For days on end we sailed over this prodigious river of a current, making our way amid thousands upon thousands of tunny migrating towards the lagoons of the remote Tuamotus. Steering at night was a bitterly cold task at times, but the sea was splendid and our boat, sailing with a Force Six wind, advanced inexorably towards our goal.

There followed nineteen nights of watching the Southern Cross, which was our guide to the island of statues, nineteen days of the sea, the waves, the work aboard, the sails that had to be watched constantly, the frequent astonishment of a brilliant sunrise, sometimes the anxious stress of night with the sea growing steadily rougher, and again and again the vast torpor of a world that was never made for men at all—a world that conjures up so many dreams for those who vainly long for adventure. What a wonderful account others might write about those days at sea, with their heavy weather, dead calm seas, and the dawn rising over the islands.

15

Our log-book shows as I leaf through it: '21 January 9.45 savage squall: nine turns on the mainsail roller-reefing gear. The jib-sheet broke.'

In the evening of February 2 our captain told us that Te Pito No Te Henua, the Navel of the World, would probably be in sight at dawn. From the point of view of sailing we had accomplished a very fine run under canvas, linking the Galapagos archipelago with Easter Island in nineteen days in our thirty-ton ketch; but we had also proved that it must have been possible for more primitive craft to reach that island within a period that would allow their crews to survive the voyage.

We spent a last night of watching, an unforgettable night in which we waited for the sign of the first birds. Then, in the midst of furious squalls, dawn tinged the horizon, and all at once through the driving rain there rose the high, shadowy coastline. Then the rain swept furiously across the sky and we lost sight of the land.

Rising fast, the dawn tore the iridescent clouds apart, showing the tall outline of the Poike plateau soaring up from the waves, a huge fire-tortured cliff-face of cellular lava and trachyte rising more than a thousand feet above the prodigious surf that tirelessly hollowed out its underwater caves.

The wind was so strong that it battered the rain-squalls into transparency, and through them, more and more clearly and in all its wealth of colour, we could make out the land of solitude, whose wonderful mystery we may never fully understand.

Slowly, feeling for the wind that turned and eddied near the cliffs, we ranged along the southern coast, which grew more distinct and then opened out in all its savagery. The hills and valleys of the empty land showed gently in the calm light, and we coasted along a shore edged with spouting waves, a shore so close yet so indefinable in its overwhelming gravity. Not a human being was in sight, not a house: only bands of wild horses and armies of sheep.

As the sun came up we doubled the cape of the

Rano-Kao volcano, which was marked by three little islands inhabited by sea-birds; and as we all stood on deck, with the heavy swell heaving under us, we felt as though we were in some uneasy dream.

So we sailed along to anchor off Hangaroa, where the wind died away. There were sheds, a few trees . . . and then that great feeling of surrender which comes when a struggle is over.

With a harsh, quick rattle we let go the anchor in thirteen fathoms. There was a strong swell, but over the water the smell of land reached us. All was still . . . the stillness of Sunday; and on Easter Island this was the time for mass.

Half the world lay between us and that Paris where we had so longed to see the face of this island, and yet it was much like everywhere else—a little flag, an enormous church, some crossbred houses . . . the picture-postcard of a disappointing holiday, had we not been buoyed up by the sun and the song of the waves.

We were tired, and as happy as though we had left night behind us. Yet in a few hours we should have to go and pay our respects to the *Jefe Militar de la Isla de Pascua,* his wife, his second-in-command, the German priest (who had gone through the 1914 war, of course) and the soldiers who protected the island against the perils of modern education. A little community that had been the subject of wildly foolish dreams, like the first love one meets again after twenty years and who has nothing left to show but a ravaged face.

At last two canoes put off and came towards us. We waited, watching the men who shyly came aboard to greet us with the unobtrusive civility of Polynesia. They gave us the quiet welcome of the island and showed us the curios they hoped to sell, for they are very poor. Then all at once there was a wild outburst of delight. They had discovered that my wife was Tahitian, that we were French, and that we had come to live on their island for several months.

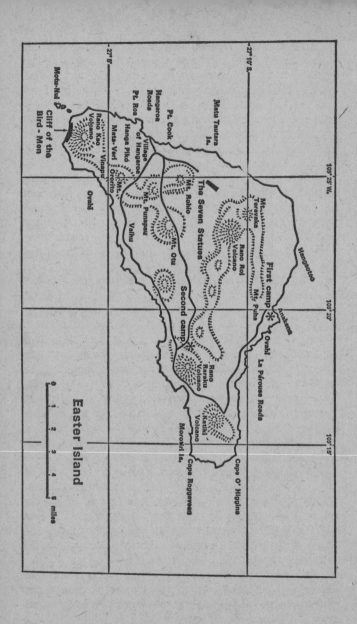

Easter Island

0 1 2 3 4 5 miles

Motu-Nui
Cliff of the Bird-Men
Rano Kao Volcano
Mata-Veri
Vinapu
Mt. Ororito
Hanga Piko
Pt. Roa
Village of Hangaroa
Hangaroa Roads
Pt. Cook
Mata Tautara Is.
Vaihu
Mt. Pumpau
Mt. Otu
Mt. Rohio
The Seven Statues
Second camp
Rano Rol Volcano
Mt. Terevaka
Mt. Puha
First camp
Hangaotoo
Anakena
Ovahi
La Pérouse Roads
Cape O' Higgins
Rano Raraku Volcano
Rano Raraku (Katiki) Volcano
Motoviri Is.
Cape Roggeveen
Ovahi

27° 5'
27° 10' S.
109° 25' W.
109° 20'
109° 15'

Following the natives' advice we changed our anchorage, for the bay was dangerous. The weather looked as though it would stay calm, and we hurried ashore in their canoes, which ran through the breakers and passed between the rocks of Hanga-Piko. A magnificent landscape opened before us. Between two flows of black lava lay a little harbour in which the natives kept their miserable canoes; and all around stood horses, cropping the meagre grass, their manes streaming in the wind. Here and there fragments of broken, defaced statues gazed at us with the same astonishment as the inhabitants. For the call had reached the huts and caves in which the Easter Islanders live. From every side we saw women and children coming towards us, bareback on their lively horses. Everywhere the island had come to life.

How lovely it is, Easter Island! It might be Ireland on the verge of autumn: and how sad it is, the gaze of these men and women who know they are not permitted to leave.

'*Ia orana oe!*' they cried—the great greeting of the Polynesians—and now as soon as they knew we were French it was a competition to see who should be the first to embrace us and who should have us stay. Presently almost the whole population was gathered round us, but I noticed uneasily that there was not a single one of the Chilean authorities. The natives explained that the Jefe Militar and the priest had just taken communion and were now having breakfast.

What did it matter? I was in a hurry to find a house where my wife could rest and I accepted the first invitation. All the natives wanted to have us and to give us their houses, which are so poverty-stricken and so beautiful in spite of their poverty. For the nine months that we were to live on that island we lived solely among the islanders, and it was a wonderful life.

Scarcely had we reached Estevan's house before crowds of these delightful people hurried in, bringing us little presents and asking my wife innumerable questions about Tahiti and all the other Polynesian islands, for they dream of them as one might dream of freedom. Thanks to their kindness we were very soon able to work out the way we should live—housing, horses, supplies for our base camps and for the boat, which had to have two boat-keepers perpetually aboard, for by a singular omission the government that occupies the island has never seen fit to build the slightest hint of a port in all the eighty years it has been there.

Very soon, too, we should have to pay a call on the governor, the military commander of the country, and on the priest who spoke of himself as 'the king of the island.'

When the time came, these officials gave us a friendly reception. The governor, a lieutenant-commander in the Chilean Navy, greeted us with all the civility that comes from isolation, and told us that our arrival had been expected for close on a year. It seemed difficult for the military mind to grasp that a yacht sailing from Europe might take several months longer than forecast. The governor assured us that he was happy to welcome us and that he would help us in every way he could; nevertheless he briskly set about giving us notice of Easter Island's very particular position.

'You know,' he said, 'that Easter Island has a special status of its own. Our island is Chilean territory, entirely controlled by the Chilean Navy, which administers it—and which I have the honour to represent.'

We were at once told that I was not to pay the natives more than the tariff that had been drawn up; that I was to ask for a circulation permit for every worker to enable him to move about the island; that during the time of my stay I should be responsible for all sheep-stealing perpetrated by any natives working for us; that I was to inform the governor of our plans for work; that I was not to give the natives wine or spirits; that I was not to allow any native women aboard; that I was to give notice of all movements of the boat; that I was to beware of the natives, who were thieves and liars . . .

and that obviously it would be as well if I were to get in touch with the priest who knew everybody, who had christened everybody, and whose one delight was archeology. Finally, I should have to put in another request for authorization to excavate, for he had received none.

As there was only one ship a year, this all seemed extremely difficult; or, to be more precise, extremely inconsiderate towards us.

'But apart from that, which, as governor, I am obliged to warn you about, everything will run smoothly. After all, we're all Latins.'

After this came a long conversation about Chile, which I had learnt to love, and which, it seemed, was the only 'wholly white' country in South America, the only one where there were no Indians any more—in short, all Latins! I thought of the last Indians of Tierra del Fuego—dead!

We had still one more visit to make: we were to call on the priest, who would surely turn out to be a wonderful man in this island, so near to God and so far from the city's din.

A concrete shed topped by a concrete cross, at the foot of which lay the greatest man of the island and maybe of all Polynesia—the man whose name was Eugène Eyraud and who came from France to give his soul to God and his life to these men of the land of silence. Eugène Eyraud was a white man; yet he brought kindness and gentleness; and here he remains.

We looked at his artless little tomb, which stood there facing the west and which bore the finest, the noblest of epitaphs:

Easter Island
To Brother Eugène Eyraud
Who, from being a mechanic, a workman with machines,
Became a workman for God,

A U T O R I Z A C I O N.

AUTORIZASE a Zelma TUKI pakarati para que pueda ir al campo, objeto
XXXcocinar al Sr. Maziere a contar del 18 de Agosto hasta fines de
Septiembre.

Isla de Pascua, 17 de Agosto de 1964.

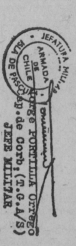

JEFATURA MILITAR
· ARMADA ·
DE
CHILE
ISLA DE PASCUA

Jorge PORTILLA Orrego
Ten.de Corb;(T.G.A.S)
JEFE MILITAR.

DISTRIBUCION
1. Interesado
2. Arch.J.M.

*Permit, compulsory for all natives who wish to pass through the gates of the village of Hangaroa to visit any other part
of the island, even if only for a few hours. This permit was issued to the islander who accompanied us as cook*

And won this land
For Jesus Christ.

A century ago. A wasted century.

We still had to pay our call on the missionary Sebastian Englert, who was by no means a mechanic. We went in. A little haven of peace, carefully maintained in the state of untidiness beloved of old bachelors—a real learned man's room for a period novel. With his little piercing blue eyes and his widespread arms Father Englert welcomed my wife and me. Speaking perfect French, tinged with that slightly grating accent that is sometimes so disturbing, he came forward. 'How happy I am to welcome you! I am so very fond of France—I stayed there two years in 1914. I lived at Roubaix and at Leuven too: you say Louvain in French, I believe?'

This fact, this recollection of conducted tours astonished me. Just as I was astonished to find myself recalling the burning of the Louvain library.

'Above all, Monsieur Mazière, do nothing without asking me; I can help you; I know everything about the island's archeology. And above all do not believe the natives—they are such liars and thieves.'

'Forgive me, Father, but have you never been able to change their state of mind in thirty-four years of pastoral care?'

In this small, isolated, forgotten, imprisoned country conditions which might border on the ludicrous elsewhere are positively tragic. The law of silence and restraint has been forced upon these Polynesians, who dream of living free and who deserve the attention of everyone for whom racialism is a crime. Even in this too isolated island, peopled by lost Polynesians, the spirit of the Conquistadors has left waste products behind it whose stench is sometimes unbearable. Yet visitors seldom write or speak of the surviving inhabitants of the island, just as they for their part never make themselves heard.

The Tragic History of Easter Island

We must give a short account of the comparatively recent history of this island at the world's centre before we can turn back into its fabulous past.

Although the buccaneer Davis spoke of land in this latitude in 1686, it was not until 1722 that the Dutchman Roggeveen, commander of a squadron of three vessels, discovered the island, which he christened 'Easter' in honour of the holy day that preceded the discovery.

On the day Roggeveen's ships arrived, only óne islander ventured oñ board: he was given presents, and this decided a great many other natives to come out to the ships. According to the Dutchmen, there was some thieving. In the afternoon the Dutch landed a company, and suddenly there rang out the cry that was to mark Easter Island's tragic history, 'Fire! This is the moment!' Many of the natives fell, including the first who dared visit the ship. As was so often the case, the arrival of 'civilization' was marked with blood.

Before they left the Dutchmen caught a glimpse of the stone giants; they took them for clay—ample evidence of their lack of any real interest. Roggeveen's account might have been of the first importance, but its poverty is such that it does not even mention whether any of the statues had already fallen.

It is probable that in 1769 the French Captain de

Surville, of the Pondicherry Company, called at the island in his ship the *Saint-Jean-Baptiste:* he speaks of it as lying in latitude 27°30′ South. Unfortunately we have seen no account of this voyage.

In 1770 the Viceroy of Peru, Don Manuel de Amat y de Jumyent, fearing that the French might settle on the island, sent a man-of-war commanded by Felipe Gonzales y Haedo and a frigate to take possession of it. There was a solemn procession and three crosses were set up on the little hills on the Poike plateau. A formal act of possession was endorsed by the natives, who did not know how to write, of course; but—an interesting detail—one islander signed with a Rongo-Rongo letter representing a bird (a character in the Easter Island ideographic writing). This is important, for it leads one to suppose that at that period the writing of tablets was still flourishing.

In 1771 and 1772 the Viceroy of Peru sent two other expeditions, and this allowed the detailed mapping of the island, which was named San Carlos. These expeditions appear to have been properly and conscientiously carried out, but we do not have the information they obtained.

Two years later the natives welcomed Captain Cook with great boldness and delight. Once more there were thefts, and once more there was gunfire. Cook notes an interesting fact: some of the statues he saw were standing and others had fallen; this gives us an approximate date for the decline of the island's art and religion.

In 1787 the Comte de La Pérouse, who was in command of the French expedition, anchored for twenty-four hours off the island; his mind was imbued with the tact of the eighteenth century and his relationship with the natives remained friendly. In spite of several thefts not a single shot was fired. La Pérouse was a true Frenchman and a man of culture; he did not consider the theft of a sailor's hat an adequate reason for killing one of the islanders: on the contrary, his gardener handed out seeds, plants, goats and poultry. Nearly two hundred years after he was there the natives still remember La Pérouse, and they call the bay in which he anchored after him—a remarkable sensitivity of memory.

In 1804 the Russian ship *Neva* visited the island.

In 1805 the crimes began again. The captain of the American schooner *Nancy*, of New London, reached Easter Island with the intention of capturing hands to go sealing. After a series of odious exactions, he succeeded in kidnapping twelve men and ten women, these latter being intended for obvious purposes. After three days at sea the chained prisoners were released on deck. They all instantly leapt into the sea to return to their island. The skipper hove-to and lowered the schooner's boats to take up the prisoners, but as soon as the boats came near the islanders dived, avoiding them. At last, weary of the struggle, he abandoned them. The murderer's account observes that some swam north and others in the direction of Easter Island.

This was a warning for the people of Easter Island, and it was heavy with consequences. In 1806 the crew of the Hawaiian brig *Kaakou-Manou* was prevented from landing because of the recent aggression. Other vessels appeared in 1808 and 1809. In 1811 there occurred another tragedy, when the American whaler *Pindos* put in. The boats went ashore to bring back water, fresh vegetables and women. They came back with as many girls as there were sailors. After a night during which the sailors proved themselves equal to their own idea of virility, the wretched girls were put back into the boats and when they were near the land forced to jump overboard. The sailors stayed at their oars, roaring with laughter at the sight of the girls swimming with one hand and clutching in the other the wretched present awarded each for the night's activities—activities whose deadly infection they were to retain for ever. It was then that Waden, the mate, took up his rifle and fired into the unhappy band. He was a crack shot, and the crew cheered him as he fired. What can one do but tremble with fury at the mentality of a murderer of this kind?

In 1816 came the Russian ship *Rurik,* with the great Franco-German romantic poet von Chamisso aboard. Seeing that the natives were exceedingly agitated, Admiral Otto von Kotzebue gave the order for everybody to return to the ship. It was a great pity that the painter Choris, who was in the *Rurik,* had no chance to go ashore and leave us evidence that might have had exceptional value.

The years passed, and one after another the ships came in. One was the French sailing-vessel *Le Cassini* which called in 1862. When her commander, Captain Lejeune, returned to Valparaiso he persuaded the Picpus Fathers to evangelize Easter Island.

A few months later the greatest of all the dramas took place. On 12 December 1862 a fleet of six Peruvian ships appeared in Hangaroa Bay. Their intention was to kidnap the men and carry them off to slavery in the then flourishing guano quarries off the coast of Peru. These same slaving ships had just attempted a raid in the Tuamotu archipelago, but they had been pursued by the French guardship, and one of them had been captured. Having attracted the people by displaying a quantity of tawdry wares, Captain Aiguire began his work. Eighty of his gang surrounded the unhappy natives, threatening them with rifles; the islanders, armed only with wood and obsidian spears, fought hopelessly and about a thousand of them were captured. Among them there were the last of the learned men of the island, King Maurata and his family.

The natives remember the event to this day, and they speak of the wailing of the prisoners, bound like animals, the death-agonies of the women and children who had been shot down, and the panic-stricken flight of the survivors, who fled to Rano-Kao, where their pursuers killed them. Hatred for the Peruvians is still so strong that when a Peruvian came to visit the island in the yearly boat from Chile only a little while ago, the threatening attitude of the people compelled him to go back on board.

Because of the crime of this handful of murderers the oral tradition of Matakiterani all but perished, to be recovered only in tenuous fragments by means of anxious research.

A few days later the Peruvian flotilla, with its cargo of bitter unhappiness, set course for the little island of Rapa, with the intention of doing the same there. The Rapa islanders defended themselves bravely, and the natives managed to capture one of the ships; it was taken to Tahiti, where its crew was brought before the French court and imprisoned. When this became known the French government, urged on by Mgr Tepano Jaussen, Bishop of Tahiti, instructed the French consul at Lima, M. de Lesseps, to intervene with the Peruvian government. England also protested, and in Valparaiso M. Eugène Eyraud, who was later to become the apostle of the Easter Islanders, aroused public opinion and offered his services to bring the survivors from their prisons.

Alas, communications were so slow that by the time the Peruvian government had ordered the liberation of the wretched slaves imprisoned on the Chinchos Islands more than eighty per cent of them were already dead from ill-treatment, undernourishment or disease. The hundred-odd survivors were taken back to their country with a tragic lack of medical supervision and they nearly all died of smallpox during the voyage. Out of a thousand prisoners only fifteen came home; and when they got there they brought the mortal infection with them.

Ravaged by smallpox, more than half the surviving population of the island perished within a few months, turning the country into an indescribable charnel-house. When he was there some ten years later it was possible for Pierre Loti to write, 'the paths are littered with bones, and whole skeletons are still to be seen, lying in the grass.' Of the five thousand people who had lived on the island, no more than about six hundred were left.

In May 1863 the schooner *Favorite* brought six natives back to the island; with them there came Brother Eugène Eyraud, and he, showing wonderful courage and sensitivity, won over the unhappy survivors to the religion of Christ. The little nation had suffered deeply, and the last upholders of the ancestral beliefs had just disappeared: the islanders quickly adopted this new religion which, through the mouth of Brother Eyraud, brought them a little gentleness.

Other missionaries followed to carry on the solitary work of Brother Eyraud, who died on 14 August 1868, having baptized the entire island.

In November 1868 the *Topaze* put in and took away the remarkable statue called 'the Wavebreaker' for the British Museum. In the same month Father Zumbohm reached Easter Island, bringing with him domestic animals and plants that might be acclimatized. And in the same year Captain Dutrou-Bornier arrived, settling on the island to raise livestock.

In 1870 the Chilean escort-vessel *O'Higgins* arrived, sent to draw up a detailed map of the island and study the customs of the islanders. This year saw anarchy engulf the island once more. A furious enmity had sprung up between Dutrou-Bornier and Brother Roussel. Shots were exchanged, huts were sacked, men were killed and wounded. Faced with this state of affairs, the Catholic mission decided to leave the country, together with the people, and to go to Mangareva. One part of the population went with the priest and another, numbering about three hundred, entered into the employment of Brander, Dutrou-Bornier's former partner, who took them to Tahiti. A hundred and eleven natives were obliged to stay on the island with Dutrou-Bornier, who was very soon murdered.

In 1871 the Russian ship *Vitias* paid a scientific visit, but in view of the desolate state of the island the Russians went to Tahiti, where they saw the Easter Islanders who had taken refuge there and where Mgr Jaussen gave them a famous tablet as a present.

In 1872 *La Flore,* a French corvette, appeared, having aboard the famous French writer Pierre Loti, who took a lively interest in the customs of the survivors. Loti's extraordinary clarity of vision and his sensitivity enabled him to write so luminous an account that in my opinion it is the finest work ever written about Easter Island. Loti took advantage of being in Easter Island to carry away a colossal head that is now in the Musée de l'Homme in Paris.

In 1875 came the second voyage of the Chilean *O'Higgins.* Then, in 1877 a remarkable Frenchman, M. Adolphe Pinart, came to study Easter Island. Like Loti, he collected many objects that were later to be the pride of the museums. He wrote an outstanding, highly detailed account of his journey.

In 1879 a man half Tahitian by blood, a descendant of the royal house, came to settle on the island in order to manage Dutrou-Bornier's property. He arrived with a team of Tahitians and he remained for twenty years; his gentle, understanding conduct won the people's love —they recognized in him the Polynesian soul. It was he who brought the passionate love of Tahiti and the Tahitian speech into Easter Island.

In 1882 the German ship *Hyaena* put in, bringing two research workers who carried out some interesting surveys of the Orongo houses and took back many objects for the German museums.

In 1886 the American Thomson, working for the Washington museum, reached Easter Island aboard the *Mohican.* He published a very well-informed book and took his museum an unbroken statue and some painted flagstones.

In September 1888 the Chilean captain, Don Policarpo Toro, suddenly arrived to take possession of the island for his country, and in the most free and easy manner he very soon granted the English company of Williamson and Balfour the right to exploit the land. So Easter Island was no longer to belong to men but to sheep; and that is the state of affairs even now. Furthermore, intensive sheep-breeding has done the greatest damage to the land and to the sparse remaining vegetation.

The natives were cooped up in the village of Hangaroa: it was surrounded by a barbed-wire enclosure with two gates in it, and no one was allowed to pass through them without the permission of the Chilean military leader. At six in the afternoon these gates were locked, for no one was to move about the island by night, except in the case of an exceptional authorization. These regulations have remained almost unchanged. When we arrived the population of the island consisted of 47,000 sheep, about 1,000 horses, 1,000 cattle, about fifty Chilean servicemen, and, in 1964, 1,000 surviving Easter Islanders living in the most unbelievable wretchedness and lack of freedom.

In 1914 the island authorities decided that any theft of sheep should be punished by fifty days of forced labour. An abortive revolt burst out, led by the priestess Anata. That same year six German cruisers put in for an untroubled call, after they had shelled the civilian population of Tahiti without the slightest motive.

In 1915 a most exceptional woman, Miss K. S. Routledge, carried out a remarkable ethnographic survey, and her papers are still of the first importance.

After this several scientific missions came to stay on Easter Island. The most outstanding was the Franco-Belgian mission of 1934. It was led by that great and lamented scientist Alfred Métraux, who wrote this harsh account of evaded obligations—an indictment that we, alas, can only confirm: 'The island lives in such a degree of wretchedness that it is impossible to speak of transition from a primitive state to our civilization. Easter Island, neglected by the Chileans or disastrously influenced by those men who are sent there, has not fallen into decadence: it has simply rotted in the midst of hopeless destitution.'

The long martyrdom undergone by the men of Easter Island helped us, during our months of research, to understand the people's sensitive state of mind and their sometimes childish dread; but above all it allowed us—my wife, my companions and me—to feel the most intense affection for these islanders, who took us into their poverty-stricken houses and their hearts and, in the teeth of racialism, brought us hope. Do not let the Chileans who read this book suppose that we are attacking their country, which has given the world such men as Vicente Huidobro, Pablo Neruda and Lucho Caseres: all we are doing is to ask them to understand that what is in question here is a quality known as honour.

It was among the natives that our life took shape. Since we were accepting the hospitality of their dwellings, we also owed it to ourselves to share in everything; and since they were so utterly destitute it was impossible for us to live for ourselves alone. We cannot accept the common opinion of passing travelers who take a pleasure in saying that these unfortunate people think of nothing but stealing. What would anyone do in the same position?

For our part we never had any reason to complain of the behaviour of the islanders; their only failing is that they have never received any education whatsoever from those who have assumed the responsibility for this island.

The authorities see fit to insist upon one day of compulsory labour a week; they think it right not to give the unhappy islanders identity papers or passports, to forbid them to leave their island, and to harass them for countless petty reasons. They are guilty of the most serious offence in the world: they have not respected the dignity and freedom of those they call "Indians,' who are the descendants of those who left us the artistic treasure of the gigantic statues and who died of other men's smallpox.

They molest the natives, they molested us too during our scientific research; yet they, who fought for their own independence, should never forget that the blood of the Conquistadors is a taint. They showed my wife, who belongs to the noble Polynesian race, the most disastrous image of what we white people are trying to preserve.

The break of day, with the sun giving the shadow of the great statues their full value and the wind echoing in the hollows of the caves, allowed us to step out into this island world where, because we could speak the language, we were to be told so many strange and unexpected things, unknown before.

We owed the greater part of our investigation to my wife, who listened with untiring zeal to life stories, sometimes told in the almost inaudible breath of the old men, gathering accounts that will disturb researchers; and doing so under the watchful eye of an interpreter whom the authorities had strongly recommended because of his morality, his loyalty and his steadiness in religion.

Our work was to be divided into two parts. My wife was to stay at Hangaroa, where all the people are penned, to carry out her linguistic and ethnological inquiries. She was also to see to the supplies that were to be sent once a week to our base camp. My English friend Bob Terry, three islanders and I were to carry out our researches over the whole of the island; and more particularly we were to set up two base camps, one for a month at Anakena and the other for four months close to our excavations at Rano-Raraku.

THREE

The Land that Died

The map of the island—a simple, beautiful map—shows a lava triangle with sides fifteen, eleven and ten miles long—47,000 acres of moor ravaged by wind and sheep, with three extinct volcanoes at the corners, marking the high points of the island.

In the middle is a windy desert that has been inhabited only intermittently. Around the edges, in the places where the land has slid away, at the opening of the caves and among the fallen statues, there are paved walks that lead into the sea, sunken gardens, rock-carvings, stone houses, the traces of former life. Here, as everywhere else, the Polynesians dwelt close to the sea.

Our first certainty was that our island, Matakiterani, was peopled about six hundred years ago by Polynesians whose origins we would try to discover. All the archeological and ethnographic data agreed, and so did the remarkable studies of Miss Routledge and Alfred Métraux.

That evening, in our camp at the foot of the *moaï* [an Easter Island word meaning stone statue] that the Norwegian expedition of 1956 had set up again, we listened to the living word; far away, at the other end of the island, my wife was to hear the same legend from the old leper Gabriel Veriveri. He is the only person whose name I shall quote in this book. He has no feet, no hands, and his face is frozen by his disease; he is forsaken, and a slow death is the only danger that hangs over him now, with his poor eyes turned towards that land of Hiva he has dreamed of all his life—my wife will never forget his dim, misty eyes when he spoke of the so-called heathen world. Was it indeed Veriveri, one evening when we were looking at the stars, who told me—and his words frightened me—about those men of the other world whose bodies are vividly striped with veins on the surface, men whose tradition brings knowledge?

That is where the whole problem lies. Veriveri will die a leper in Easter Island, just as I have seen the forgotten pygmies die. He will not be believed because he has a skin whose colour 'civilized' people copy once a year at great expense: he will not be believed because he does not speak the same language—he speaks gently. For when he spoke to me he looked into my eyes and I recognized his truth. When in former times the initiates of Matakiterani spoke, men were required to listen in silence. We white people write digests without having digested the history of our origins in the very least. I have no idea of where I come from.

Veriveri's island has two strange names—Matakiterani and Te Pito No Te Henua: where do they come from? My country is called France; another is called Chile; still others USA and USSR, like the call-letters of a telephone number. A name is a light, a clue to the meaning that can only be properly pronounced by those who are in love, and I know that Veriveri is wildly in love with the land, with the waves and the stars.

'King Hotu-Matua came to Easter Island in two canoes,' said Veriveri. 'He landed at Hangaroa, but he gave the bay the name of Anakena, because it was the month of July.' Now the only way of taking advantage of the winds that blow from Polynesia to Easter Island is to travel in July and August. This very small detail is the first important aspect of the tradition. Why should this Polynesian king take refuge in this uninhabited country? Was it a consequence of one of those civil wars that are so very frequent in history? Here is what the tradition says:

'King Hotu-Matua's country was called Maori, and it was on the continent of Hiva. The place where he lived was called Marae-Rena . . . The king saw that the land was slowly sinking in the sea. The king therefore called all his people together, men, women, children and the aged, and he put them into two great canoes. The king saw that the disaster was at hand, and when the two canoes had reached the horizon he observed that the whole of the land had sunk, except for a small part called Maori.'

The tradition is clear: there was a cataclysm; and it appears that this continent lay in the vast hinterland that reaches to the Tuamotu archipelago to the north-west of Easter Island.

Another legend, handed on by A'ure Auviri Porotu, the last of the island's learned men, says this: 'Easter Island was a much larger country, but because of the sins of its people Uoke tipped it up and broke it with a crowbar . . .' Here too we have a cataclysm.

A more important point is that according to tradition Sala-y-Gomez, an islet some hundred miles from Easter Island, was formerly part of it, and its name, Motu Motiro Hiva, means 'small island near Hiva.'

We have three signs pointing to this cataclysm. Yet generally accepted geology does not acknowledge any vast upheaval in this part of the world, at least not within the period of human existence. However, there are two recently discovered facts that make the possibility of a sunken continent seem reasonable. When the American submarine *Nautilus* made her voyage round the world she called attention to the presence of an exceedingly lofty and still unidentified underwater peak close to Easter Island. And secondly, during his recent studies carried out for the Institute of Marine Resources and the University of California, Professor H. W. Ménard not only speaks of an exceedingly important fracture-zone in the neighbourhood of Easter Island, a zone parallel to that of the Marquesas archipelago, but also of the discovery of an immense bank or ridge of sediment.

Apart from preserving the memory of these upheavals, tradition also states that King Hotu-Matua came from the west. Now in Easter Island on the Ahu A'Tiu there are seven statues, and they are the only ones on the island that look towards the sea, and, more exactly, the western sea. Their precise placing might well fix the area of the cataclysm, which would thus lie between the Marquesas and the Gambier islands. It seems probable that during one of those sub-oceanic upheavals still so frequent in the zone between the Cordillera of the Andes and the New Hebrides, an archipelago—I do not presume to say a continent—may have sunk or been altered. Moreover, according to Professor Métraux's findings, it seems possible that King Hotu-Matua's men emigrated from this area of the Marquesas; the reasons for believing this are based on linguistics—the use of the word Hiva is an example—and many points of ethnological agreement. The date of this migration, according to the genealogies that we collected, would be towards the end of the twelfth century.

This settlement in no way excludes the possibility of other contacts at far earlier periods—contacts that we shall speak of later.

Tradition says that Hotu-Matua decided to leave the land of his fathers at the first sign of earthquakes, but that he first sent out seven explorers, all kings' sons, to search for that Navel of the World whose position had been revealed to him by Haumaka's dream. This leads us to suppose that if the subsidence of a continent did occur, then it was at a much earlier date, for Easter Island already stood alone in Hotu-Matua's time, and he reached it only after a very long voyage by canoe.

Yet it is strange that if such an upheaval did take place, the legends of the Marquesas islanders should not have preserved the memory of it in unmistakable terms.

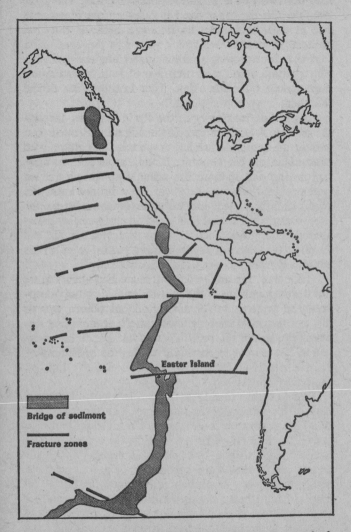

Map which could explain the disaster which, according to Easter Island tradition, overwhelmed the continent of Hiva

I do not know of any, except one ambiguous Mangarevan tale. On the other hand it seems to me impossible that Hotu-Matua's men should have distorted tradition to such an extent. Everything points to the conclusion that the disaster was confined to certain archipelagos, which would by no means prevent it from assuming an importance of the very first order in the minds of the islanders.

As with all the history of the Pacific Islands, the origin of their settlement remains confused and open to a variety of interpretations. It is certain that other men reached Easter Island before Hotu-Matua, and we have the clearest evidence of this. King Hotu-Matua's seven explorers said that before leaving they did not know the origin of Ngata-Vake and Te Ohiro, who had been the first to come to Easter Island. According to the information handed down to old Veriveri by Hanga A Tuakava A Oviri, 'very big men, but not giants, lived on the island well before the coming of Hotu-Matua.'

Those were the only records that we had at that time; but it was quite certain that what they told us only deepened the mystery of Matakiterani. Our course was to pay the closest possible attention to the records that tradition had handed down to us; and we already knew the tale of the seven explorers and the legend of Haumaka.

FOUR

The Legend of the Seven Explorers

'A man called Haumaka dreamed, and his spirit went to Matakiterani. First it touched at the three little islands that stand at the foot of the volcano Rano-Kao and it called them "the sons of Te Taanga." ' (These were nephews of Haumaka's in Hiva.) 'Then his spirit ran over the crater of the Rano-Kao volcano and named it "Haumaka's dark hole." Then it set off to explore the island, searching for a bay where King Hotu-Matua might land. As it travelled towards the Poike plateau, at the far end of the island, it came across some kohe plants, and broke off a shoot. Then, having looked over all the bays in the island, the spirit stopped at Anakena; and seeing such beautiful sand it cried, "This is the place, and this is the great bay where King Hotu-Matua will come and live." Then going back to Hiva it said, *"Towards the rising sun there is an island; and you will go and live there with King Hotu-Matua."*

'Seven kings' sons, all initiated men, set off to explore the island and to make ready for the king's coming. Their names were Ira, Raparena, Ku'uku'u A'Huatava, Rinirini A'Huatava, Nonoma A'Huatava, Uure A'Huatava, and Makoi Rinirini A'Huatava.

'They came from Hiva in a single canoe, and following Haumaka's directions they went past the three little islands and put in at Vinapu. Then they climbed the volcano and cried, "Here is Haumaka's dark hole!"

Then they set about planting the yams they had brought with them. Ku'uku'u planted them.

'Then they went towards the eastern shore and on their way they found the kohe plant that Haumaka had trodden upon and broken. When they had gone along the Poike cliff they made their way down the northern coast, looking for a bay with a little sand, so that the king's canoes might run ashore. But all the bays seemed impossible as landing-places. So they went to fish at Anakena, and there they cried, "This is the beach where king Hotu-Matua will land!" They could find no fire, so two of the explorers went to their canoe to fetch it. They brought back makoi wood, made a fire, heated volcanic stones and cooked their fish.

'While they were eating they saw a turtle coming up the beach. It was a spirit-turtle. When it saw the seven explorers coming to take it, it tried to reach the sea again and it took refuge on a rock on the beach called Hiro-Moko. Ira was the first to try to grasp it and to turn it over. They all tried, and none could seize it. They they asked Ku'uku'u, the last, to try. When he made to grasp it, the turtle struck him violently with its flipper and left him for dead. His six companions laughed to see Ku'uku'u in this state and then carried him into a cave, while the turtle went back to Hiva.

'Ku'uku'u said to his companions, "Do not abandon me." They replied, "We shall watch over you," and they set about building six little stone mounds to which they said "When Ku'uku'u calls us, answer for us, saying, "We are here." Then they went away towards Hangaroa, leaving the unhappy Ku'uku'u alone.

' "Are you there?" he called, and the mounds of stone answered, "We are here." He called in this way many times, and then he died.

'Ira and Raparena stood on the Hangaroa rocks watching the breaking waves. Ira said to Raparena, "Ruhi is on the right hand, Pu on the left—a necklace of pearls round the throat of the Moaï [statue] Hinariru. There is another at Te-Pei in our land of Hiva."

'From the bay of Hangaroa they climbed the Rano-Kao volcano and went to see their field of yams at Orongo. Weeds had grown up. They plucked them out and said, "This land is bad."

'They built a hut to sleep in. Makoi said to Rinirini, "Stay awake when I ask Ira and Raparena to repeat what they said on the rocks of Hangaroa, for you must stay here alone when we go back to Hiva." When night came, Makoi said to Ira and Raparena, "What did you talk about at Hangaroa?" Raparena answered, "Why do you want to know?" Makoi said, "Because I want to know." Ira agreed and asked whether Rinirini were asleep. Makoi pushed him with his foot and Rinirini pretended to sleep. Then Ira said, "Ruhi on the right hand, Pu on the left, a necklace of pearls round the throat of the Moaï Hinariru."

'Rinirini heard and rejoiced, for he would be able to steal a pearl and show it to those who were to come and live with him on that island.'

There are several details of particular interest in this extraordinary legend. Apart from the fact that the seven explorers brought fire and makoi wood in their canoe, four other points seem to me important:

1 When they were in their own country of Hiva these men knew about the making of stone statues. 'A pearl necklace round the throat' gives us a valuable pointer, for pearls are found only in the Tuamotu lagoons or those of the Gambier islands.

2 Five of these men went back to Hiva.

3 They brought yams.

4 We also know from the exact descriptions of places, not all of which I have recorded here, that Easter Island had the same topography that it has today.

Furthermore, the account confirms the poverty of the island's vegetation at that time.

FIVE

The Coming of King Hotu-Matua

We are also very well informed about the coming of King Hotu-Matua and his settling in the island. The legend says:

'One day Hotu-Matua's two canoes came in sight of the three small islands called Motu Iti, Motu Nui and Motu Kaokao. Rinirini, who had stayed on the island by himself and who was watching at Orongo, saw them, and when the king called out "What is this land like?" he answered, "It is a bad land: the weeds grow over the yams." Then the king cried, "Ours is a bad land too: there is wretchedness there also. The high tide will destroy everything."

'Then the two canoes separated. Hotu-Matua's went round the island eastwards; Queen Ava-Reipua's went round it westwards. They met again at the opening of the bay of Anakena and each canoe went towards one of the two rocky headlands that bound it. The king went to the point called Hiro-Moko; the queen landed at that called Hanga Ohiro. As soon as she was ashore the queen bore a daughter, while in Hotu-Matua's canoe a son was born to Vakai.'

Right next to the bay there are dry caves and a spring, and this must have made life possible for the little band, which, seeing that the canoes were about a hundred feet long, would not have numbered more than two hundred. The plants and the animals were taken ashore at once. We know the kinds: there were yams, taro, bananas, ti, sugar-cane, coconuts and sandalwood seedlings, and probably young breadfruit-trees too. Only the rats and the poultry had survived the voyage but it appears that the emigrants had also carried pigs. It is also possible that the seven explorers had prepared for their coming and had planted crops, thus enabling them to survive.

One must try to imagine the arrival of these colonizers, exhausted after their prodigious voyage, 'having left a country of trees and of warmth' as the legend says, and finding this deserted land, swept by the cold wind.

Two essential elements were about to vanish for these Polynesians—the coconut-palm and the breadfruit-tree, the very basis of their diet. For these trees cannot bear in this latitude: no more than two coconut-palms have lived, and they are sterile. Only the bananas hold out in the shelter of the sunken gardens, of which we shall speak later.

Although by far the greater part of the island is no more than a vast conglomerate of puffy lava, the small amount of earth that lies upon this crust is of excellent quality, and vegetables, such as the *kumara* [the sweet potato], which is the present basic food, do exceedingly well on it. The crops were planted with pointed sticks, which were called *akauve* or *oka* according to their size and which were used to make holes of a greater or lesser depth.

The island's great difficulty is raising trees and keeping them; for since the soil is no more than eighteen inches deep their roots are obliged to run almost horizontally. Because of the great strength of the winds, trees had to be protected by drystone walls, and one often finds these round *manavai,* ten to fifteen feet across, in the neighbourhood of the houses. In these shelters, which are reminiscent of the protective walls in Ireland, there grew the following kinds of tree, which have now all entirely or almost entirely disappeared:

the toro miro, a remarkable wood that was primarily used for sculpture; the hau-hau, whose fibre was used for weaving ropes and fishingnets; the mahute, whose bark was used to make the cloth that we call tapa in Polynesia; the marikuru, whose seedpods made necklaces; the maunau, whose fruit was the people's basic diet in time of famine. The islanders made scent out of its wood, and the children used its nuts to make spinning-tops. And lastly there was the makoi, a wood with a very beautiful grain that was used for carving. There is nothing left of this tree, or of the mahute, except a few very wretched specimens.

All the earlier travellers spoke of the perfect arrangement of the plantations, and at the time of the island's discovery Mecklemburg, the ship's clerk with Admiral Roggeveen's expedition, wrote: 'Everything there was planted, sown and tilled, the strips of land separated from one another with great precision and the boundaries perfectly straight.'

In this country without animals agriculture at once necessarily took a most important place, and there is no doubt that Hotu-Matua's first care was to divide up the land and to mark it out very exactly with the little cairns of stones that are still to be met with all over the island.

Hotu-Matua's men must have competed with one another in hard work and spirit to make this harsh land habitable and to accustom themselves to it. It is likely that their first dwellings were the caves that are to be found everywhere; they would have lived there even before they built the canoe-huts, those marvels of adaptation to the furious winds, whose stone bases are still to be found.

SIX

A Pilgrimage in Time

It was from the canoe-huts that, on that first evening, there at the far end of the pink Anakena beach, we began our long pilgrimage towards the island's spendid past. Every day, as soon as our troop of horses had left the beach after the morning swim, we stepped into the realm of silence. All around us was the evidence of this dead past—the traces of the canoe-huts on the ground and embedded in it, unbroken, those wonderful cut stones that supported the roof. These houses in the form of an upturned boat had extraordinary small door-ways, and in front of these doorways was still to be seen, quite undamaged, the half-moon of paving that once served as a resting-place.

Where did these huts come from? Were they a memory of the first canoes turned upside down on the shore of this inhospitable land? Were they a surviving traditional technique, the same as that which is found in the Marquesas?

Where did that primitive yet subtle, refined society come from—the society which lived in these huts roofed over with turf and plaited *totora* [a kind of rush that grows in the island's volcanic craters], and which created the great sculpture of silence?

We sought it everywhere, in the underground galleries and on the floors of caves littered with chips of obsidian and the remains of food; we sought it on the slopes of the volcanoes where, like tombs, there stood the ancient marks of a cultivation that has wholly perished. We sought it among the cliffs that are so eaten away as to be almost inaccessible, where men had nevertheless taken refuge.

Sometimes this Navel of the World seemed to be a hiding place for demons, whose abstruse signs were cut into the rock all over it. Every day we explored ten caves or more—there are hundreds of them on the island. In their galleries our torches lit up the faces of Make-Make or of Aku-aku. Some of them still had traces of that wonderful flame-coloured paint that the women used as a cosmetic.

It is these sparse, violent traces that are so disturbing on Easter Island. Matakiterani is not dead: she has been blinded by the brilliance of a thousand suns. We began to feel that what we had here was the umbilicus of a serious, dignified civilization, and that the navel was not its beginning but its end.

We sensed the frontiers of an awareness that we should be unable to cross, for it may be that it was on Easter Island that the most violent shocks had taken place, those that release the connections of a different kind of consciousness. Often, when we watched the night sky with my native friends, the name Ure Ti'oti'o Moana would recur; and that means meteorites. There are three of them, deeply buried in the island's soil, and the natives know about their fall. The last came down not ten years ago, on the horizon, and the sea rose up, playing havoc with the Anakena beach. They spoke about the long trail it had left in the sky, and they told a strange legend, that of Rani-Topa, the sky falling.

'In the days of Rokoroko He Tau the sky fell.
Fell from above on to the earth.
The people cried out, "The sky has fallen in the days of King Rokoroko He Tau."
He took hold: he waited a given time. The sky returned; it went away and it stayed up there.

Once again Tonga-Riki was given a name—Rani-Topa.'

Sometimes these legends are so solemn that no one has dared to write them down.

'He took hold: he waited: it went away and it stayed up there.'

It may be that these statues of the volcano, of Mataki-terani—'eyes that gaze at the sky'—were carved in order to keep watch on the wildness of those nights lit by the stars, some of which let fall these blazing drops. And the eyes of the god Make-Make, those enormously enlarged eyes, are they not the eyes of men taking shelter in the caves? Why reject these possibilities after two hundred years of archeology on this scrap of land have yielded nothing? We were going to live four months under the shadow of the statues, and we were going to accomplish a journey with them quite unlike that of merely taking measurements.

Every day we rediscovered these statues, which we called the Others because they are of a different style altogether from those we had seen at first. Their backs are turned to the sea and they stand over the *ahu,* those great stone platforms that watch the life of the villages. These statues and these alone have open eyes, for they were set into the tombs where the dead were buried. There only, after the statues had been brought from the quarries, did the sculptors open the eyes: the moaï were the embodiment of a reality, and they were then given the great red tufa cylinders that capped their massive heads.

Alfred Métraux thinks that these cylinders, these *pukao,* represented the head-dress of the former natives —splendid red turbans of the dead; and they were topped by a small, sometimes white, cap that resembled the head-dress, but which perhaps also symbolized here, as it does elsewhere, that place in the skull through which the Asian and African initiates believe that knowledge is received and which we call the fontanelle.

All these statues have fallen face downwards and the

caps of knowledge have rolled a great way off, leaving the flat, bald crowns uncovered. In falling they have opened the stone tombs in which there lay the time-whitened bones of those who had been the Ariki, the kings of a little world in which men gave birth to giants.

All round the island, and almost always on the seaward limits, are these stone platforms called ahu, some with no statues, others of various classes and in all stages of preparation. The island has about 240 of them—a prodigious number.

The humblest are the 'ahu without moaï', which belong to the decadent period, the time of the end of this Navel of the World, when the work of the initiates was wrecked by overcrowding and disease. By then it had been many years since the quarry of the giants had heard the stone-cutters' song.

There are platforms of every kind—semi-pyramidal, usually small, in which the handsome inclined plane is lost in the general form; rectangular, which are somewhat higher, with their burial chambers hidden under the rubble; and then those strange platforms called *Ahu-Poépoé,* which resemble narrow launching-ramps standing over the sea. They belong to a completely different art: perhaps they might have revived this form of burial, but they were the last, the seven last, before the Peruvian massacre. And there are others, as huge as the statues that dominate them. These number about a hundred, fifteen of them wonderful and three unforgettable, placed as though to guard the three corners of the island's triangle. Their names have a splendid ring, like the roll-call of the past—*Ahu-Vinapu, Ahu-Hekii* by La Pérouse Bay, and lastly *Ahu-Tongariki,* at the foot of the quarry-volcano Rano-Raraku.

To provide some idea of the whole, let us give these proportions: a façade of upright exactly-joined stones about two hundred and sixty feet long and ten high—this façade always facing the sea. Between this line of masonry and that which runs parallel to it—thus forming a kind of stage some ten feet wide, composed either of rubble or of pounded stone—there are to be found the burial chambers called *avana*. Above them lie very fine slabs of stone six to ten feet in circumference, and upon these rest the bodies of the moaï. Behind this great wall, and facing inland, there is a gently sloping courtyard, very carefully paved, with either polished or cut stones, two parallel wings, and farther to one side a rectangular construction of gravel and pebbles held in place by masonry. This is where the bodies were placed until they were completely dry: then the bones were collected and put with the skulls in the burial chambers of the ahu. All this is typically Polynesian; but in the case of Ahu-Vinapu and Ahu-Tongariki the outstandingly precise and special architecture gives rise to certain unavoidable hypotheses. There is no doubt that Ahu-Vinapu is an anomaly in Polynesian architecture. We are perfectly familiar with the stones and slabs of worked coral set up edgewise that are the glory of the Marquesas and Raiatea *marae*: but we must emphasize the strangeness of this Vinapu architecture, which accords with some of the very exact canons of pre-Inca building. Faced with such phenomena one cannot reject given hypotheses; and it is certain that the red tufa statue that the Norwegian expedition of 1956 raised up in the court of the ahu gives a great deal of food for thought.

For my part, I do not regard this statue as wholly Polynesian, and that is where the crux of the problem lies. The same applies to the basalt statuette that we found in a secret cave at Hotu-Iti and whose photograph faces page 48.

The clues are tenuous, but they cannot be set aside. Heyerdahl's views have met with determined opposition, but we cannot reject everything out of hand, especially since the thesis of contact between Polynesia and South America is supported by the great scientist Paul Rivet. It may be that that is where the great problem of Easter Island lies. There is a place called the Navel of the World near Tihuanaco. Who can say whether South

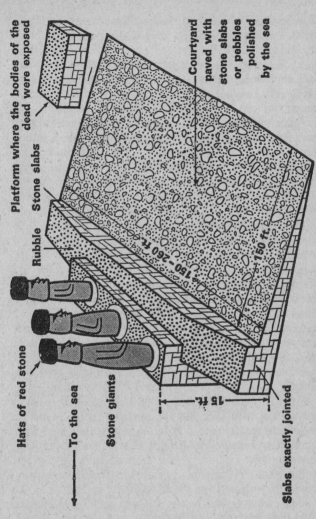

Platform where the bodies of the dead were exposed

Stone slabs

Rubble

Hats of red stone

To the sea

Stone giants

Slabs exactly jointed

Courtyard paved with stone slabs or pebbles polished by the sea

150 ft.

150–260 ft.

75 ft.

Plan of ahu-moai, the stone platform on which the giant statues were set up

America, as the result of some extraordinary contact, did not give this island its name—Te Pito Te Henua? Why not?

We have spoken at length of the history of Hotu-Matua because the evidence is there and it is tangible; but we believe that there were other men before Hotu-Matua.

The whole of the Easter Island legend is confused by the fact that there were two races living there together at the same time, the Hanau Momoko and the Hanau Eepe, who have been called 'the men with long ears'. Many authors accept this interpretation, but we do not —there is a phonetic error. In fact the natives still say *eepe,* and not *epe,* whose exact meaning is 'stout' or 'strong' men. Since the expression Hanau Momoko is translated as 'the weak (or weakened) men', the most probable version of Hanau Eepe is surely 'the strong men'.

All this emphasizes the presence of two different races. Yet all the writers quote the evidence of the first travellers. Roggeveen's official writer says, 'Some of them had ears that hung down as far as their shoulders and some wore two balls in them—white balls as a mark of great embellishment.'

These statements are certainly exact, and they are natural; for if these natives came from the Marquesas this was the usual custom there at that time.

This was in 1722, and the narrator adds, 'Some of the inhabitants served the idols more often and with greater devotion and zeal, and this led us to suppose that they were priests, all the more so since they wore distinctive marks, having not only the large balls in their ears but also their whole head shaved.'

There were both Hanau Momoko and Hanau Eepe upon Easter Island. According to tradition, the Hanau Eepe came in the time of King Tu'uko'Iho, who, some say, reigned a little after the death of Hotu-Matua, thus assuming a royal character that he did not possess to begin with. And these two races lived side by side, intermarried, built the ahu, and finally plunged the island into civil war—the war of the two leagues, which was to bring disaster.

Tradition says that Tuu Maheke, Hotu-Matua's successor, went back to Hiva. Contacts between eastern Polynesia and Easter Island were set up, and it is not impossible that the second wave of long-eared migration merely consisted of the descendants of Hotu-Matua's people, allowing for the mixture of Melanesian and Polynesian blood that first came into being in the Marquesas archipelago.

It is likely that the Hanau Eepe left Hiva as the result of a war, for the legend states that they came without any women—hence the mixing of the two strains on Easter Island, a fact that renders any serious anthropological study impossible in our day.

May not Ahu-Vinapu represent the evidence and the basic pattern of an art conveyed to Easter Island by earlier contacts—contacts of which these Polynesians were aware?

There is one aspect, quite apart from the purity of its architecture, that attracts attention at Ahu-Vinapu: the stones of its façade are slightly convex; and I am not aware of any comparable example in Polynesia.

There was one islander, and one alone, who told me some very strange things about the Hanau Eepe; I do not know whether his information is to be believed, but it is so important that I cannot leave it out. He said: 'The first men to live on the island were the survivors of the world's first race. They were yellow, very big, with long arms, great stout chests, huge ears although their lobes were not stretched: they had pure yellow hair and their bodies were hairless and shining. They did not possess fire. This race once existed on two other Polynesian islands. They came by boat from a land that lies behind America.'

What is one to think of an account of this kind, an account that threw a patient investigation into confusion and sometimes compelled us to change our scholastic attitude?

With the exception of the Catholic missionary Sebastian Englert, who has written a studious book on the island's traditions, I do not know of any expedition staying on Easter Island that has had a perfect knowledge of the native language. Only my wife spoke the tongue of the islanders of former times with complete ease. How can it be expected that a native, communicating in pidgin-Spanish, should reveal traditions that need days of respect and friendship to be mentioned at all?

Surely taking the easy way in a scientific enquiry is wrong. Surely the straightforwardness of rejecting no source of information that comes from the natives' heart and friendship is right.

When Dr Paul Rivet, the director of the Musée de l'Homme, published his views in favour of contact between Polynesia and South America there was obviously a great deal of controversy; but the precision and good sense of what he maintains required that we should look closely into his argument before we entered upon our own island adventure.

From what he says it is evident that there are decided points of agreement between the Polynesian languages on the one hand and those of Tierra del Fuego and of the Aymaras of Ecuador and ancient Peru on the other: many expressions are exactly the same. Great numbers of elements of their culture are common to them all, and there is a strong resemblance between most of the customs of these peoples—the division of society into castes, the conjunction of temporal and spiritual power, the use of a ceremonial language different from that which is commonly used, similarity of feather ornaments, division of property, human sacrifice and cannibalism, and so on.

As Pierre Honore says, 'These Urus, the first dolichocephalic inhabitants of South America, spoke the Arawaks' language, and they built their huts in the coves and on the islands of the great lake. The area in which they lived stretched from the first slopes of the Andes almost as far as the Pacific. Their vessels, which were made of reeds and which, according to the specialists, came from the region of the Amazon, are identical with those we see in the sculpture of Easter Island . . . This comparison of the mysterious Easter Island writing with the scripts of the Indians and the dwellers on the Pacific coast is not so paradoxical as might be supposed at first sight.'

Alfred Métraux notes that 'The pictographic system of the Cuna Indians contains a whole series of symbols identical with those of Easter Island'—yet we have never carried out a serious study of this similarity.

The clues come together all over Easter Island. We have discovered dolichocephalic among the brachycephalic skulls. And then again there is that astonishing legend which was collected by Eugène Caillot in 1912 and whose sources I have searched for ever since I found this note in a Mangarevan dictionary compiled in 1860 by the first missionaries: 'Anua-Motua, the father of Teagiagi, came from the Hawaiian Islands and went off to Easter Island (Matakiterani, but before he did so he left several children borne by his wife Kautia at Mangareva. He died on Easter Island. His sons Puniga and Marokura, and for a certain time Teagiagi, dwelt on that island, which he left to them . . . '

SEVEN

The Prodigious Voyage of
King Anua-Motua

In the reign of King Taratahi an Avahiki chief called
Anua-Motua came from that country with his family
and his warriors to settle in the Mangareva islands. He
came on a single raft and first he touched at Taravai, at
a place called Agakono: the hut in which he and his
family lived was called Popi. He stayed at Taravai for
quite a long time and then went to live in Gatavake
[Mangareva] at a place by the name of Teauragi; it
was the main centre and in those days there were more
huts built there than anywhere else. His family was exceedingly numerous. In the end this disturbed Taratahi,
the King of Mangareva. Seeing Anua's family growing
larger and larger and taking on importance because of
its connections with other chiefs in the archipelago, he
first decided to declare war on Anua-Motua and to destroy him or force him to go away. But having thought
for a long time he said to himself, 'Anua-Motua is a
much stronger man that I am: if I fight him, and his
warriors too, I shall be beaten, and I shall have caused
many of my subjects to die uselessly. It is therefore better that I should go away with all my people, of my own
free will.'

And indeed he set out directly with his people upon
rafts, and he left the Mangareva islands without any
hope of seeing them again. Besides, some time before
he left, Anua-Motua had spread the rumour that if

Taratahi did not leave Mangareva for ever, he, Anua-Motua, would crush him and his people. The unhappy king had therefore made the most prudent choice, if not the bravest.

Taratahi no longer being there, Anua-Motua proclaimed himself king of Mangareva. His power was further increased by a most important submission. When the *aretoa*[1] Kipo, who was then the leader of the warriors of Taku, learnt what Anua-Matua had done to Taratahi, he came at the head of his warriors to acknowledge Anua-Motua as ruler; for he did not wish to share Taratahi's fate. The other chiefs and their followers in all the other parts of the archipelago did the same; they too declared themselves Anua-Motua's subjects, and this meant that in fact the different islands had but one master.

From that time onwards Anua-Motua was the king of the Mangareva islands. He was rid of all his rivals and he reigned peacefully over the archipelago for about fifteen years. At the end of this time he once more felt a deep longing to travel. He wanted to make a great voyage towards the south. Furthermore, he was urged on by the wretchedness of the people, who had grown too numerous: there had already been a great many when he came to the archipelago, and their numbers had never ceased growing. That year there was a terrible famine: there was hardly anything for the people to eat. One day Anua-Motua's son Teagiagi, whom he had made high priest, said to him, 'Father, you did wrong to expel Taratahi from his land: see how wretched we are now. Let us go and find Taratahi.'

His beloved son's idea, together with his desire for new adventures, determined Anua-Motua to leave, although he was no longer young. So he caused two great

---

[1]Title given at Mangareva to warriors who had distinguished themselves in battle in a quite extraordinary manner; it meant courageous, strong, powerful—almost the same as the title of hero.

rafts to be made, and went aboard them with part of his family and his people, fifteen hundred persons altogether. Then, having proclaimed his grandson Rikitea king of Mangareva and having set up one of his sons, Hoi, as king at Taku, he left the island of Mangareva and sailed towards the south-east. It is said that at the moment he vanished from sight there was an earthquake at Mangareva: the people who had remained on the island thought that Anua-Motua was bound for the land of the gods.

The first island that Anua-Motua's expedition reached was Oeno [also called Teauotaneoi by the natives of former days]. He and his people very quickly saw that it was uninhabitable. They at once set off again and landed at the island Eiragi [Pitcairn], which like the other was uninhabited in those days. Anua-Motua decided to people it. He made his daughter Tuatutea, who was married to Tiniraueriki, queen, and left them a few warriors and women as subjects. Then he took to the sea again and came to a high rising land like that of Makatea; this was Puapuamouku [The Elisabeth Island of today: it seems that the earlier Mangarevans called it Kairagi for a while], and it too was uninhabited. There, says one Mangarevan tradition, Anua-Motua left his daughter Pigahere as queen, with many of the expedition's people. But another says that to begin with Anua-Motua meant to leave his daughter and a few people at Puapuamouku, but finding no vegetation or fresh water on the island he was afraid his daughter and the others might die of hunger, so they all went back on board and carried on with their voyage. However that may be, Anua-Motua and most of the emigrants did not stay but went on over the sea. They put in at Kooa [Ducie Island: another Mangarevan name for it was Tekava], where they did not remain long, for the island had nothing to offer them. They then steered for Matakiterani or Kairagi [Easter Island, also named Rapa-Nui and Te Pito Te Henua by other Maoris], which was the main goal of their journey.

The voyage was long: the days went by, and no land appeared at all. The people on the two rafts were filled with dread. Anua-Motua alone was unmoved, together with his sons, for they trusted in him—they knew that their father had travelled all over the world and that he must therefore know the way to the island. Anua-Motua and his three sons, Teagiagi, Puniga and Marokura, were all on the same raft; and it was steered by the sons. However, the voyage stretched on and on past measure, and at last its length filled the high priest Teagiagi with anxiety. Yet he did not dare say anything to his father, at whose side he usually sat in the bottom of the raft. But very early one morning he climbed to the highest place on the raft and there—surprise!—on the horizon he saw a great black mark that was nothing other than high land seen from afar. He at once went down to tell his father, who, followed by his other children, came at once to see what showed in the distance; and his head was wrapped in the kind of sack called *tupata* [a sack that was made in those days from the leaves of the *hara* (pandanus)]. Anua-Motua was cold: everybody was shivering. Looking up at the stars Anua-Motua reflected for a moment and then said to his children, 'We must turn back: we have almost reached Taikoko.' The sea was extremely rough in this place and the air was more than keen: it was piercingly cold. His children asked why they were not to go forward any longer and Anua-Motua told them that the farther they went the colder they would grow, and that in that direction there were two stretches of land with a dangerous sea between them; he told them that the name of that sea was Taikoko[1] and that the part of it where small but strong and evil waves never ceased breaking was called Ragiriri[2]; he told them that there was no vegetation at all to be seen on the land along the sea, that the sun was not high

[1]Tai — sea close to the land: koko — way out. This, it appears, would have been the sea off Cape Horn; and the Mangarevans say that their ancestors were very well acquainted with it.

[2]Ragi — sky: riri — angry.

—that is to say, it never rose far up in the sky—that there were tall barren mountains, cramped narrow valleys and an open piece of sea with many whales in it and particular kinds of fish that were not to be seen at Mangareva.[1] He added that he had passed that way, coming from Avahiki to Mangareva, but that at one time he had thought he would perish there; and it was for that reason, because it was dangerous, that they were not to go any farther forward.[2]

Then he fell silent, and in obedience to his words his children hurried to put the raft about: seeing this, the people on board the other did the same, and the emigrants began a new voyage in the other direction. Fortunately for them this one was not so long as the first, and the east winds blew them quickly towards the island they wished to reach. At last, after a reasonably good crossing, they came to the island Matakiterani or Kairagi. They were all exhausted and they were at the end of their resources. Now Anua-Motua said to his son Teagiagi, 'Go on shore and see whether there is anyone on the island.'

Teagiagi obeyed: he reached the beach, and from there he went up into the inland country, which he

[1] It seems that this would have been the Le Maire strait, unless perhaps it was that of Magellan, in Tierra del Fuego.

[2] If Anua-Motua passed by here in coming from Avahiki he must have come from the south-east, which is opposed to the claim of the other Maoris of eastern Polynesia, who state that they came from the west. I therefore know nothing more important in all the Polynesian traditions than this account of Anua-Motua and his children: it is filled with exact and interesting detail and it shakes everything that has hitherto been laid down and maintained by the learned as to the western origin of the Polynesians. Yet after all it may be that what was true for some Maoris was not for others—that some may have come from Avahiki or Havaiki in great numbers by way of the west, and others, a few of them, from the east. But in that case one would at least have to know whether it was a physical possibility for them; and for that one would have to know the exact position of Avahiki. In fact, however, we have no knowledge of where that famous region, land or island lay.

searched in every direction, but he did not meet with any human beings whatever. At last, when he had wandered for hours and hours in every part of the island, he came to a little dried-up stream. In this place there were a great many dead bodies and bones.

Anua-Motua's reign on the Island of Matakiterani (Easter Island)

Fortunately for the emigrants the first harvest was successful. The next was good too, and the others were still better. The people therefore no longer had to fear the evils of famine, and indeed quite soon the country was abundantly well supplied.

Anua-Motua lived for a fair number of years after this, reaching a great age. All his life he remained the master of the people, feared and obeyed by them and by his children and grandchildren, who stayed about him. Yet he had a very deep affection for them, above all for Teagiagi, his favourite son. He had dedicated him to his god, and Teagiagi was a powerful man in the eyes of the people. But Anua-Motua's children knew that behind the father there was the king, who would never, as long as he lived, allow his power to be taken from him; and half out of affection, half out of fear of being disinherited, they took great care not to anger the famous old man.

One day when they were all gathered in his hut one of them, Teagiagi, said to him, 'Father, who will you leave your kingdoms to after your death?'

The old man thought for a moment and then answered in these words, 'I give Mangareva to my grandson Rikitea; Tuatenukura—that is to say the region of Taku—to my son Hoi; Kiriau [Kirimiro] to my son Rerei; Agatai-Nui at Koro [Gatavake] to my son Ipo; Taravai-Magamaga to my daughter Ruaga; Tekoamaruhia-Takiama [the headland of the great channel] to my daughter Monogi; Magaoe [Atituiti] to my daughter Pure; Akamaru Ratue to my daughter Anuaiti; Magatirokavi [Aukena] to my daughter Tope; Eiragi to my daughter Tuatutea; Puapuamouku to my daughter Pigahere; Matakiterani to my sons Puniga and Marokura.'

Then he felt silent and his family understood that he had uttered his testament. There was a deep silence in the hut for some moments while each of the children thought about the share of the inheritance that had fallen to him.

Teagiagi seemed downcast: all through the sharing of his father's possessions his face had displayed intense surprise. Finally he stood up and said to the king, 'Father, no doubt you have forgotten me: you have given all your possessions to my brothers, my sisters, and the son of my dead brother Matagiakaparo. Do you then leave me nothing?'

'My child,' went on the old man, 'I have left you far more than I have left them, since you have all the rest of the horizon. Go, sail away and you shall come to possess a far larger country than theirs: I promise you the land of Temomonamua.¹ It is divided into two parts: the smaller, together with the little islands that are not very far away from it, is to be for your brother Mamarape; the other, which rises before and which is a huge country, I have kept back for you—it is that country which shall be your kingdom.'

Mamarape was a child that Anua-Motua had had at an earlier time with a woman called Marape; the child had died young and his spirit accompanied Teagiagi wherever he went: for Anua-Motua he was a distinct component of his family.

Teagiagi thanked his father very much indeed for his kind provision for him and withdrew, together with the other children. Not long after that Anua-Motua died. His hut was used as his grave.

The king's children took possession of the lands he had left to each. Puniga and Marokura began their reign

¹It seems that this word may mean the rest of the world, the remaining space.

over the island of Matakiteragi. Yet Teagiagi did not at once go away in search of the country his father Anua-Motua had promised him: it was very painful to him to leave Matakiterani, since so many memories held him to it, and for a certain time he stayed. As he now no longer owned anything he withdrew and lived with a private person name Taioko. It was with extreme amazement that the people saw the high priest reduced to this humble state, but he did not complain. And in spite of everything Teagiagi went on helping his two brothers Puniga and Marokura cultivate their land. Each of them wielded the axe and the pick to clear the ground: they all worked together. But Teagiagi knew that Puniga and Marokura disliked him and that they were only looking for a chance to get rid of him: he was afraid that any moment he might see them raise their tools to kill him.

In the end, therefore, he grew tired of this dangerous state of affairs and he told his two brothers of his decision to leave the island together with some of the people —those who had been put directly under his orders and who were to be his future subjects. Puniga and Marokura took care not to try to hold Teagiagi and his people back, for their going would free them from a continual uneasiness as to their future plans.

So Teagiagi, his daughter Tahiko and about two thousand people set off on rafts and steered towards the east.[1] Mamarape's spirit went with his brother Teagiagi upon the raft, which was carrying the body of his father Anua-Motua. He was taking it, he said, to help him find the great kingdom that was to be his.[2]

From that moment on nothing more is really known of Teagiagi and his companions. The Mangarevan tra-

[1]According to some natives it was necessary to pass by way of Taikoko-Ragiriri to go to Avahiki and to the promised land of Temomonamua, and this was the direction Teagiagi took after the death of his father Anua-Motua.

[2]Another version says that Teagiagi, accompanied by the spirit of his brother Mamarape and carrying the body of his father Anua-Motua, left Matakiterani almost alone on a small raft.

ditions about them are vague and contradictory. One of them confines itself to observing that he and his people never left any sign of their passage anywhere. Considering everything, that is the most likely outcome. Yet there is another legend—much less widespread, to be sure—which runs as follows. The vessels with Teagiagi and his companions aboard wandered for a great while upon the surface of the sea and the travellers had much wretchedness to bear. The hardship almost killed Teagiagi's daughter Tahiko. But one day when she was exceedingly thirsty and she asked her father for a coconut to drink, Teagiagi suddenly saw a splendid country rising on the horizon—it was the land of Temomonamua, which his father Anua-Motua had promised him. At last he made a happy landing there with his companions and they all settled in that country. It is thought that he died there.

The details are precise and exact, and as far as we can rely upon tradition, the value of this legend, which seems to me of the very first importance, should not be underrated.

Was Anua-Motua's migration before Hotu-Matua's or after it? We cannot say. But what if the one were an extrapolation of the other? What if they were in fact the same?

In Mangarevan *motua* means father-god, and in the Easter Island language *matua* has the same force. Still more important is the meaning of *anua* in Mangarevan —cold, fog. Anua-Motua is 'the god of the cold'.

How strangely this description of going by way of Taikoko coincides with that of Tierra del Fuego!

So what we have been thinking during more than ten years of research in the Pacific may be true. Men from pre-Columbian America may indeed have reached Polynesia and civilized it—for tradition says that those men who appear so mysteriously in the Polynesian pantheon, Tupa, Tiki . . . came from the east. This unexpected knowledge provides fresh lines of insight.

Eugène Caillot translated the legend of Anua-Motua

in about 1912; at that time no serious research had been carried out on Easter Island. So there is not the slightest possibility of an adaptation of another legend. The very ancient tradition of the Mangarevan islands was still unbroken, and Caillot did outstanding work upon the Mangarevan genealogies. How could that tradition have inherited these precise names for those icy regions?

Throughout the whole extraordinary tale of Matakiterani we should never forget the entirely abnormal geographic and climatic situation of this isolated scrap of lava upon which, without the slightest transition, there arose the strangest and most hermetic art and writing in the world.

Some research workers, who are acquainted with the esoteric tradition that remembers the changes in the earth's axis[1], are disturbed by the fact that Easter Island, at certain periods within a few miles of the magnetic equator, should have at the far end of its own exact axis that small area of land whose name can easily be seen on the map and whose renown is preserved by the greatest of traditions. But there is no doubt that although our Easter Island informants did not presume to answer certain exact questions or were unable to do so, they did possess a knowledge of the Antarctic lands. Old Veriveri talked to us for a long while about former countries that are now covered by the Antarctic ice. On that utterly remote, isolated island it was wonderfully moving to hear men speak of a country that we have only just begun to discover. The details are precise: in the midst of these lands, he said, there rises a great cliff of red rock, and the rock holds certain powers. It is impossible not to be disturbed by knowledge of this kind.

---

[1] An angle of 23°27' between the equatorial axis and the plane of the ecliptic.

EIGHT

The Initiate King

So we lived on at Anakena, trying every day to push aside the shadowy curtain that veils Easter Island. I remember those starlit nights when my native companions told me about the life of the island and about the death of Hotu-Matua, whose memory lives on like that of a golden age.

'Grown old and feeling death upon him, Hotu-Matua called his children together. He spoke to them and shared out the island, thus bringing the different tribes into being. Then he said to his children, "Stay like this, close to my head, close to my feet and close to my body; and you, go and fetch me clean water for the last time, for when I have drunk it I shall die."

'He drank the water and said, "Pay heed to my last words: I am going to call the king of Hiva, our land." From the top of Rano-Kao, turning towards the land of his birth, he cried, "E Kuihi e Kuaha, just let me hear the cock crow!"

'From Hiva the crowing of the cock came back, "O'oa Také Heuheu." And so the king died.'

The island was divided into eight main tribes: the Miru, the Haumoana, the Ngatimo, the Marama, the Ngaure, the Ore O'Hei, the Tupahotu and the Koro Orono. It was then that the violent civil disagreements began. Very quickly the island separated into two leagues, the one taking possession of the west-north-west and the other of the south-east and more particularly of the Hotu-Iti region.

Although there were boundaries and although there was hatred, the men of one tribe would freely marry the women of another, and thus set up fresh alliances. This state of affairs, which arose from the smallness of the island, was also a defence against inbreeding, a danger that now haunts the minds of the descendants of the hundred and eleven survivors of the tragic events of 1862.

Adoption was a common practice, and because of that and of these cross-connections and the relationships between the tribes, the island's domestic organization was that of the 'undivided community', that is to say several families descended from brothers and sisters, for example, all living under the same roof and acknowledging the wise authority of the eldest. This great undivided family was also a very rigid hierarchy—a fact that often led to quarrels over wounded honour.

Like Polynesians, who have always won their living from the sea, the Easter Islanders built their huts along the shore, while their sharply-delineated stretches of land ran towards the interior; but it appears that the central parts of the island were never inhabited except perhaps by a few fugitives or men beaten in tribal wars.

Over all these tribes there was a king, called the Ariki-Mau and sometimes the Ariki-Henua, which means king of the world. Yet it seems that these kings were not always respected, and that during the civil wars some of them were taken prisoner. Only a few of them—Hotu-Matua, for example—seem to have possessed *mana*[1], that inner power which we shall speak of again later and which allowed them to master every situation. The king used to abdicate in favour of his eldest son when the young man married; and as early as his birth the king would transfer his mana to him.

Although we have doubts in the case of some kings,

[1]A Polynesian word meaning the force and concentrated strength that certain men possess and know how to use.

they usually lived at Anakena in a hut about a hundred and fifty feet long that stood on rising ground by the sea.

One should picture this broad inlet with its black and violet flows of basalt on either side and its crescent of pink sand swept by the wind to the foot of the ahus with their statues—a scene of calm in this land of storms. Rarely has any king's dwelling arisen in nobler, more splendid surroundings. A boundary ran round the whole area, so that no one could make his way into the royal compound, for the king's hut and his person were both taboo, that is to say forbidden and holy. No one might approach the king or speak to him without having first asked the king's servant, the Tu'ura, for an audience. No one might touch the king, and the things he owned were sacred.

It was his head that was sacred beyond everything else. He wore a great deal of hair, and no one was allowed to cut it. The sacred character of the head and particularly of the hair, regarded as the receiver and the donor of power, is a curious point which is found again and again in the mystical aspect of kingship.

A very sad tale shows the value attibuted to hair. When the last king of the island was dying of smallpox at the Catholic mission the priests wanted to cut off his hair. He refused, but he was shorn by force. He died a few hours later, and the natives still think that it was the missionaries who killed him, by taking away his mana.

This child-king had been christened Gregorio: he was eight. He was the last king, and it is still said that when he went, mana too left the island: that is why the holy turtles which were believed to be a magic link between all the Polynesian lands have never returned to the shores of the island of silence.

When the taboo king moved from place to place he was invariably carried in a litter, and here once more we find not only a Polynesian custom but also the usage of pre-Columbian America, which held that a king communicated his mana to everything he touched. This supernatural power had to be kept for the welfare of the people, who required the royal person to protect the community, the harvests, fishing, the lands, the broods of the hens and the fertility of the women. Even now, because of this power, this force of the royal head, the people still attach a very great magical importance to the possession of a king's skull. It was a singular reflection which prompted an islander to ask me why the Chileans shaved the prisoners and the soldiers, and why the priest, who had no wife, was also shaved.

Once or twice a year the king received the homage of his people, who offered him garlands of shells and flowers; and above all, he presided over the feasts at Anakena during which the newly tattooed children were brought before him, for the patterns were very serious matters and taboo. Then the children who were learning *kohau,* that is to say writing upon tablets, were brought to him by the *Maori Rongo-Rongo,* the initiated priests who, with the utmost earnestness and respect, taught the famous holy characters that we call ideographs.

The king himself, tattooed all over with the most highly wrought traditional symbols, remained apart from his people in order to preserve his mana: and this is how we picture him, the incarnation of the mana, crowned with feathers, a feather-covered poncho of *tapa* [a cloth made from bark] flung over a body blue with tattooing, living alone, apart from the queen, and attended only by a servant who was never to turn round in his presence. As we see it, this king was not so much the temporal head of the island as the living incarnation of a higher force and of a long tradition in which the people believed and which provided him with his vital powers.

The priests, chosen from the noble families, dwelt in the sacred shadow of the king; we have very little knowledge of their role, though I think it was similar to that of the Polynesian priests—'preservers and teachers of the tradition'. But it all remains very confused, for we have little information on the religion of former times—it was shattered by the carrying away of the greater part of the priestly caste to Peru in 1862.

In 1864 the first missionary, Brother Eugène Eyraud, wrote that the pagan religion was already dead. Although at the time it would have been of the greatest value to preserve the last testimonies, this investigation was neglected. From what we have been able to recover, it seems that the men responsible for holy things were called *Tumu ivi Atua,* which may be translated as 'the descendants of God', or more literally 'the descendants of God's bones'. They believed in everlasting life, and also in the return of the ghosts of the dead; these were called *aku-aku,* and they assumed such importance on the island that they still seem to be at hand. It appears that it was the priests' duty to avert (sometimes, alas, by human sacrifice) the spells and charms they cast.

But it is our opinion that the residual beliefs which the missionaries like to regard as proofs of an alarming paganism are merely commonplace, degenerate remnants of dead religions. We cannot believe that the nation which set up the statues did not at one time possess a very sensitive, complex religion. At all events we know that their religion embraced at least three important divinities of the Polynesian pantheon.

1 In a creation-song recorded by the American Thomson in 1886 we find 'Tiki, the Lord, coupled with a rock and begot red flesh. Tiki, the Lord, coupled with the sand woman and begot Hauhara.' Tiki is the creator-god of the Polynesians of the Marquesas, and Pacific mythology is haunted by his name.

2 Another legend speaks of the coming of the sea-god Tangaroa to Tongariki. He came in the form of a seal to take possession of the island. There is another remarkable and pertinent fact: one of the island's rarest pieces of sculpture represents a seal-man, or more exactly a sea-lion-man.

3 Lastly we know that in this island, which is terribly afflicted by seasonal drought, Hiro, the great god of

navigation, became the god of rain, and I think the god of fertility too, since what the natives call Hiro's rock is a huge monolith pierced with holes and carved with vulvas.

We have a very singular record that explains the transformation of Hiro, the Polynesian god of travelling by sea, into Hiro, the Matakiterani rain-god. 'The priest who was to pray for rain went up to the top of the mountain, and there he buried a piece of seaweed-covered coral. Then he begged Hiro to weep so as to restore life to the parched earth.'

This is a curious extrapolation of a sea-myth. What can have given rise to it? One has the feeling that it was a notion borrowed by another race and distorted.

In 1864 Father Hippolyte Roussel noted the survival of other deities, Tive, Rarai Roa and Haua, Make-Make's companion. With the exception of Make-Make we know almost nothing about these other divinities, who seem to me to have been deified kings—in former times this was usual in the Marquesas. But the god who dominated the Matakiterani mythology was the great god Make-Make, whose face is to be found carved in hundreds of places on the cliffs or in the island's caves, and whose memory is living yet.

For the men of Easter Island Make-Make was the creator of the world and of the first man and the first woman. Here are two legends that we collected.

The Creation of the World

> Vapours, mist, emptiness.
> The sea, the surrounding void.
> Darkness.
> The first trembling, the first word that brought
>   light into being.
> *Kuihi-Kuaha* [a magic word]
> Let the land be dry!
> Let the sea go back!

There came the great light, the sun,
There came the little light, the moon,
There came the stars,
Kuihi-Kuaha.
There came Make-Make, the first man.

The Creation of Man

Make-Make took a gourd, looked at himself, saw
   his face and cried,
'Make-Make's eldest son.'
There came a white bird,
Settled on his right shoulder,
Cried, '*Kuihi-Kuaha te anga a makemake.*' [magic
   words]
Make-Make rolled earth into a ball,
Thurst his hand into the middle of it to make a
   hole
Then breathed into the hole.
A young man, He Repa, came out of it.
Make-Make said, 'This is not right!'
He made He Repa sleep.
Make-Make took a banana-shoot.
He opened He Repa's chest on the left-hand side.
The blood flowed on to the banana-shoot.
Then Make-Make breathed into the shoot running
   with blood.
Uka, the young woman, was born.

The god Make-Make, the creator of the world and of
life, is related to the legendary characters of Tiki in the
Marquesas and of Tupa in the Gambier islands. He is
the Beginning.

But in the island of silence Make-Make seems also to
have been at the origin of an exceedingly important tradition and of a religious covenant.

NINE

The Magic Rite of the Bird-Man

According to the legend, Make-Make set out to look for sea-birds, and he put in at the little island of Motiro Hiva (Sala-y-Gomez). There he drove the birds before him to Matakiterani.

So that men should not destroy them nor eat their eggs, Make-Make settled them upon the two very small islets under the Orongo cliff, Motu Nui and Motu Iti. And these two rocks and these birds were at the origin of a cult that has no parallel, the cult of the *Tangata-Manu*, the bird-man, and of Make-Make, the god of the creatures of the air.

Although this bird-man is one of the most poetic and beautiful productions of Matakiterani art, he is even more remarkable as a clue to research. To begin with, the fact that these birds were brought to Easter Island rather like homing pigeons, messengers from the land of Hiva, and that they were at once protected by the god Make-Make, clearly indicated the importance that the islanders attached to this reminder, this living testimony of the far-distant migration from Hiva. Furthermore, we have a tradition that strengthens this view. Every year a few frigate-birds, *manu-tara,* were kept in captivity until they were fully grown. Then a band of red tapa was put round their wings and the priest let them go, saying, 'Fly, go back to Hiva.'

In former days this god Make-Make presided over

Matakiterani's most important ceremonies, and we know that his mana was so great that some natives assert that they have seen him—'His clothes were as white as a cloud, edged with rainbow.'

Once a year this god of life hallowed the extraordinary rite of fruitfulness and of a return to the beginnings which was celebrated in the astonishing setting of the Orongo cliffs, which on the one hand look on to the lake in the Rano-Kao crater and on the other at the splendour of the three little islands, opalescent in the spray. This pagan festival contained all the wonderful sense of rebirth that is to be found in the various cults of life.

The preparations for the festival began as early as the end of July. The essence of it was watching for the coming of the first birds and the taking of the first egg, the symbol of the new year and of the southern spring. There is no ceremony like it in the whole of Polynesia; and it is precisely this birth of a new cult or this recollection of an earlier one which is so disturbing.

There is nothing stranger than the search for this egg that has come from another country, from Hiva, and that symbolizes life and strength. But it is worth remembering that this symbol of the egg, the witness of the re-born spring, the bearer of life, was the symbol used by megalithic civilizations long ago in countries so remote that any parallel would border on the fantastic.

We have many accounts that tell us about the impressive magical action of this ceremony, which only came to an end in 1866.

During July the people gathered at Mataveri, at the foot of the volcano. Here there stood three huge meeting-huts built of cut stone laid in courses. The men and women of the different tribes, the chiefs and the warriors and the bird-men's attendants all met together with songs and dancing. Then in a long, long procession up the *Ao* path [Easter Island name for a dancing-line], winding along the bare sides of Rano-Kao, the men and the priests went to the Orongo sanctuary. A dream-like march, for the candidates for the title of bird-man had been chosen by the god and the visions of the priests. Crowned with their head-dresses of cock and tropic-bird feathers, their faces painted red and black and their tattooed patterns gleaming under their *hami* [belts made of tapa], the initiated men reached the top of Orongo, their dancing-line keeping the measure of the ritual song.

The candidates for the title of bird-man were to stay there on Orongo while their attendants, the Hopu-Manu, went to the Motu Nui islet.

Lastly the Ariki-Henua—the king—came and gave the Hopu-Manu the signal for starting for the rock.

It was a wonderful and sometimes a tragic feat, this swimming across the strait which lies between Orongo and the little islands, and in which the current runs with uncommon fury. First, by a path overhanging the caves and the precipices, the Hopu-Manu made their way to the foot of the enormous cliff-face of the volcano. With the stems of the totora that grows everywhere in the crater they made a conical buoy in which they put a little food. Then they plunged into the sea. Holding their buoy, or floater, in one hand, swimming laboriously against the current and keeping clear of the sharks the Hopu-Manu finally won a footing on the steep-sided islet. While they waited for the coming of the first birds and the laying of the first egg, the Hopu-Manu lived shut away in the little cell-like caves that are to be found today, decorated with faces of Make-Make and pictures of bird-men.

Sometimes the wait was long, and if the sea was rough the Hopu could not receive further supplies. They watched the flight of the birds day and night, each hoping to take the first egg. One must try to comprehend the strange experience of these men squatting in underground dens which they reached through a dark, narrow hole, listening through the thunder of the surf to the harsh cry of the birds and watching their flight as they glided with the wind.

The waiting man and the huge-eyed god Make-Make had the same expression. The Hopu-Manu was to become the transfigured man, wholly changed by the bird's return.

Far over on the Orongo cliff, high above the waves and gazing at the wheeling of the birds, the future Tangata-Manu, the warriors, the priests and the king waited for the sign from the gods. From the rocks—rocks carved with a hundred and fifty or more wind-polished petroglyphs—the traditional chant arose as the men made lavish sacrifices of the finest kinds of food so that the god should look favourably upon the search for the egg and upon the return of fruitful life. And there above all, the Maori-Rongo-Rongo priests, those who wrote the word upon the toro-miro tablets, recited the long progress of that life which perished for having believed in the return.

Sheltering high on the windswept Orongo cliff, the watchers waited for the first cry from the rock. Their splendid, dreamlike cave in the dizzy precipice of the volcano was called *Hakarongo-Manu,* the listening-place of the birds. And suddenly the cry of life would ring out, echoing back from the cliff, 'You—shave your head!' It was a Hopu-Manu on the island, perched on a rock named 'the cry of the bird', calling his new king.

Silently the man went down to the sea, and dipped the egg into it before tying it to his forehead with a ma-hute band. Then all the Hopu-Manu, surrounding the one whom the god had imbued with his strength, swam fearlessly towards the Orongo cliff. Alone among the lava screes, climbing the dizzy overhangs, the consecrated man at last reached the feet of the new king, to whom he gave the precious symbol.

As soon as the watcher had heard the name of the new Tangata-Manu and had passed it on, the chosen man, using a delicate, transparent obsidian blade, shaved his scalp, his eyebrows and his eyelashes—he became the bird-man. An initiate tied a band of red

Face of the god Make - Make

Representations of Bird - Men

tapa round his arm, and into this cloth there was slipped a little piece of sandalwood. With his sanctified arm he received the gift of the egg.

Here is a point that seems to me noteworthy—this piece of sandalwood, the emblem of kingly refinement, and above all of the homeland. For we know that it was Hotu-Matua who first brought sandalwood to Mataki-terani, there being a great many sandalwood trees in the Marquesas.

Tradition states that the new king received the egg on the palm of his hand covered with red tapa—an admirable gesture, and one that calls the nobility of the ceremony to mind. Then all the company surrounding the king—short-lived in his royalty but holy in his possession of God—went dancing and singing towards the foot of the volcano. The men, brandishing their ceremonial paddles, attended the new Tangata-Manu, who went into a trance. Our informant also says that in addition to the red and black painting round their faces the men also wore wigs made of women's hair. This is a remarkable detail, for in the Marquesas holy objects were formerly adorned with human hair or with the precious beards of aged men, and the wig was formerly the mark of the priests.

Then, at Mataveri, there were great feasts during which human sacrifices were offered. It is said that afterwards the Tangata-Manu withdrew to the Rano-Raraku cliff, which stands above the great statues. There he was to live alone for a year, leading a wholly continent life; and by the same token he was not to go into the sea. He lived in a little hut next to that of his attendant, who fed him with the daily offerings that all the people were required to bring him. For twelve moons he was the god-man, cut off from the world; he was the keeper of the mana, of the vital force of the year—a year to which he gave his name, the name that was revealed to him in a dream. In the same way the Hopu-Manu who had found the egg was obliged to leave his family for a while, and he was not allowed to touch any food with his hand, which was held to be taboo.

Some very interesting ideas emerge from this. The continence imposed upon the mana-possessing man. The withdrawal and the shutting away of the initiates. The terrifying force of the mana and of that hand, which had become as dangerous as a king's footstep— 'Mana can kill.' All these notions are to be met with elsewhere in Polynesia; but they are also to be found in prehistoric South America.

The holy egg remained hanging in the hut until the next year, when it was hidden among the rocks of Rano-Raraku.

When the Tangata-Manu died a great ceremony was held over him, and all the other Tangata-Manu came, together with the priests and the chiefs of all the tribes. Alfred Métraux mentions a very singular detail that was unknown to me. 'During this ceremony the role of the bird-men consisted of untying the ten cocks that had been bound to the dead man's toes.' How very strange a sight it must have been, this holy corpse lying on the stone platform of the ahu, its feet plumed with the feathers of these ten living cocks. A splendid interpretation of the death of the man who was the essence of the birds and one which could only have existed in this island whose eyes gaze at the sky . . . at the birds. Thus the birdman, the incarnation of the new year, of the god Make-Make, lived on in a land whose king possessed a reflection of higher forces. 'Make-Make was present in all places.'

There is also another ceremony that we must speak of; we have little information about it, but it seems to have been dedicated to this same god. After the choice of the new Tangata-Manu, the sequence of events at Orongo provided for an initiation festival that I think particularly important: this was the initiation of the children who were called the Poki-Manu. Accompanied by their fathers and most probably by those Tangata-Manu who had not won, the children, both boys and girls, went up to Orongo, their arms and legs bound with strips of white mahute tapa, bearing on their shoulders wooden *Tahonga,* which some understand as representing coconut-palms. Once they were there their hair was cut and they were given a name. They stayed in the hut called Tau-reva, in which there stood the exceedingly beautiful statue called 'the Wave-breaker', which is now in the British Museum.

It is likely that ceremonies of sexual initiation and homage to fertility took place at this time. The number of figures of vulvas on the Orongo rocks is such that it can scarcely be doubted, particularly as this initiation formerly existed in the Marquesas and most of the other Polynesian islands, especially the lengthening of the lips of the clitoris, carried out by the old women.

The picture of Make-Make has striking likenesses to certain Mangarevan and Marquesan incised drawings—the representation not of the god Tiki but of a different face, one that I met with in the Omoa valley, at Fatu Hiva.

Miss Routledge, who carried out the most thorough investigations on Easter Island, states that in 1915 she was able to draw up a list of eighty-six names of Tangata-Manu. This is a most important piece of information, since we know that the Tangata-Manu gave his name to the year. Counting backwards from 1866, the year of the last bird-man, we come to an approximate date for the birth of this fascinating form of worship. Even if we grant that some names were left out we cannot reach a higher figure than a century. On the face of it, then, we may suppose that the cult began about 1760.

A question arises: did a second migration set up this worship in Easter Island and at the same time overturn the statues? Roggeveen, in 1722, speaks of having seen the statues upright and of having noticed a flourishing vegetation. In 1770 Felipe Gonzalez y Haedo states that when he took possession of the island the assembled people uttered the cry of 'Make-Make' and that a native drew a Tangata-Manu upon the document recording the act. Yet in 1774 Cook notes the throwing down of the statues and the absence of trees and of thriving cultivation. If this second migration did take place it would certainly explain also the rapid degeneration of the religion.

We know very little about this religion, but it seems that here, as everywhere else in Polynesia, its complexity and its worldly value arise from its taboos and medicine.

The taboos it put forth provided life with an exact pattern, and breaking them might mean death. In the first place there were the taboos concerning the king— taboos to do with his person. There were others to do with the harvests, and, for example, there was that taboo to do with fishing and particularly with tunny-fishing which was forbidden during the winter months. I myself have still seen this taboo respected today; for the natives say that during these months when the tunny are migrating they give you asthma. It is likely that this taboo was imposed as a result of accurately observed facts which seemed trustworthy. New huts and new canoes could not be used until they had been seen by the Ariki-Henua, who conveyed his mana to them. There were very strict taboos about death—it was forbidden to light a fire or to fish anywhere near an exposed corpse; and it was forbidden to eat certain kinds of food after the death of a relation. There were taboos on property. And lastly there was the general taboo on the ahu.

The power of the word, the spoken word, was very deeply felt here, and once an incantation had been uttered it seemed obvious that it would make itself felt with all the strength of a broken taboo.

It is likely that the priests, who practised medicine of a kind, based on herbs, sea-weed and shells, also taught respect for the great traditions. This may be seen from the enthralling legend that we gathered from the lips of old Gabriel Veriveri.

'How a man can tell when he ought to lie with a woman.

'He must watch during the eight first days of the new moon,

'Maninao o'hua, the moon of a man's phallus.

'He must find the woman, lie with her.

'The child that is born from this coupling is worth seeing.

'A perfect child.

'These are the children who will be brought forward for the Rongo-Rongo learning, to take part in the bird-cult, to tattoo the legs of women, to tattoo the foreheads of women, to tattoo the hands of women, to tatto the cheeks of women, to carve the Kohau-Rongo-Rongo.

'What distinguishes a child born in the declining moon from a child conceived and born in the new moon is that he will be a commonplace child, devoid of understanding . . . '

Here we have the true teaching of the first religion; for in those days the sources of life were not set apart.

So our daily life went on at our camp at Anakena. Sometimes we would see our ketch come into the bay for shelter, but with the quickly-changing weather she would have to set off again for Hangaroa, or, if that was the way of the wind, she would go and lie off Vinapu.

And every day we would gallop on horseback either to the headland of the Poike peninsula or along the north coast, recording the petroglyphs or mapping the ahu. At the other end of the island my wife translated the legends and the records she had gathered. Luck always seemed to be with us, thanks to the affection of the natives.

One day an old man, a descendant of the royal line, came to see my wife and told her that if she chose to go with him in a few days' time—and if she could get him a permit to leave the village—he would take her to the north coast and give her a king's skull, which would help us everywhere.

I must be forgiven if I do not give the precise names of our native friends in this book, but in view of the attitude of the authorities towards them and in view of the fact that they are forbidden to give foreigners anything old (of course this does not apply to the Chileans: quite the contrary) I must not and will not let myself slip into any indiscretion about our friends who are still on the island.

We were fascinated by the idea of seeing one of these king's skulls at last. After we had turned and twisted a great while among the lava boulders our friend showed us a hidden cave, and in a recess within it, the ancient, secret skull. We were very much moved, but apart from that there were two things that struck us at once: the skull was dolichocephalic (long-headed) and therefore out of the ordinary run, and it had a perfect set of teeth, which is extremely rare among the Polynesians of today.

Thanks to this native friend doors now open to us, as though this skull did indeed possess mana, as he asserted. Very soon we were to learn matters of great consequence.

Thus, before we left Anakena, a friend took us to another place where, under a heap of stones by the sea, we discovered an extraordinary basalt statue about four feet long whose exceptional technique was strangely reminiscent of the Marquesan Tikis.

These first two discoveries were to point the way in our enquiries. We already realized that the problem of this strange world was about to become wonderfully complex.

In recalling these two first proofs of the natives' friendship and their courage, it is my duty to deny in the strongest terms the assertions of several writers who have spent a few days or months on the island, who have not had the courage to face up to certain embarrassing facts, and who have tried to minimize the inadequacy of their work by writing with extreme grossness about the natives, who will obviously never be able to reply.

When the islanders know how to read, and hold papers of citizenship, they will weep with shame for those who have spoken of them as thieves and liars and of their wives as loose women.

TEN

The Historical Ethnology of the Island of Matakiterani

When dawn breaks over the island nothing is to be heard except the wind and the bleating of the sheep, of which the governor takes the utmost care. There is only the wind; the wind whose sound was listened to in former times, for it brought with it life from the other islands, in dreams.

At night we often came to the Anakena beach to listen to the storyteller, and we listened as the people used to do long ago, in silence, for the word must never be broken in upon. He told of the life that he had heard about from his grandfather, who was a 'cannibal' but who still knew the song of the men who carved the statues. He told of things belonging to another world, whose paths he could no longer find.

He said: 'In the old days the children were not like this, for the Atua watched over them. In about the fourth or the sixth month of pregnancy the father-in-law would give his daughter-in-law the present of a stone oven, an *umu*. He gave her the intestines of a chicken as food to show his reverence for the child that was going to be born. The rest of the food was given to the family. All this was holy.

'When the time of birth came, the mother knelt on the ground while her husband supported her, pressing her to help her breathing and her bearing of the child. As soon as the child was born the cord was bitten through, never cut with obsidian, and it was tied respectfully, for the mana handed on by its parents was being shut into the child's body. A priest was there for the observances of the rites, which had to be very strictly followed; and the dreams he had the night before gave guidance for the child's life.'

Here again we find the full observance of the birth rituals practised among all so-called primitive peoples. Thus the umbilicus and placenta were either carefully buried or else they were thrown into the sea.. But at Matakiterani the priest uttered these words, which testify to the origin of this little nation. He cried, 'Go! Go back to Hiva.'

'Then gently warmed pebbles were put on the mother's belly to push out the last oozing, to prevent weals and to make it easier for the muscles to go back into place. A little after that the mother took her first food from her husband's hands, with all the required forms, while the baby was given his first name. Then he was to live.'

Often, sitting in the shelter of a cave while our horses rested, cropping the short grass, we would ask our friends questions. One of them knew a great deal, for his father had been Métraux's informant. Gazing over the distant sea, we asked him to tell us about the children and their life.

'In the morning the children used to go and play in the waves; they tried to glide on them with their arms stretched out or on bundles of totora. [This game, now called surf-riding, was formerly current throughout Polynesia.] The mothers watched over the little ones on the paved forecourts of the huts, showing them how to play with the tops made of stone or the shells of the naunau-tree nuts. Others practised the bird game with mahute tapa kites stretched on makoi wands.

'After the meal, which everyone took together round the *umu* [a stone oven that was made to glow with heat: the food was put into it wrapped in banana leaves, the whole being covered with earth], the children either went with their parents fishing or working in the gardens, or else they practised throwing stones or toro-miro spears, while others straddled banana trunks and slid down grassy slopes.

'Before sunset the parents taught the children the ritual game with string; its tradition has been preserved, and it is called Kaikai. The game consisted of making various figures with a loop held between the two hands; on Easter Island the figures were extremely complicated, and they had to call to mind some event or some exact image. While the figure was being built up, the player was to chant the ritual words that went with it. It was not merely a game; it was also a form of memory-training, a preparation for learning the Rongo-Rongo writing, which conferred honour on those who came into contact with it.

'These games went on until the age of puberty; and in the old days this was not a halting-place but a point that the young people passed by with the utmost freedom. It was a time for a great deal of idleness and for the coming together of the girls and the boys in the big huts called *hare-nui,* where dancing and other delights were taught.

'The children used to help their relations in the various kinds of work when their help was needed. That is how things were in time of peace. When there was war, the children had to take refuge in the cold darkness of the caves, where many of them died of hunger.'

In this same way, at night, we heard of the ancient custom of not lighting a fire. This is an exceedingly interesting custom, and one that even now causes the old people to say that a light is a bad thing, one that kills the power of seeing by night. We often thought of those children hiding in the dark caves; yet they walked about in them quite easily. The old men still say that formerly people could see at night and that in the caves they could make out everything perfectly well. They say that if one is used to the darkness from childhood and if one never makes use of a light at night, one's eyes, like those of the animals, can see in the dark. It is true; and it may explain many archeological mysteries.

What is more, a few days afterwards we discovered some strikingly well-executed wall paintings in an underground gallery more than a hundred yards long. Now no trace whatever of fire could be seen on the ceiling of this minute gallery, and although when we searched the floor we found the remains of meals, we could not detect the least sign of burnt wood, any more than such traces can be found in the famous painted caves at Lascaux.

The whole of this early life that seems so idle at first glance was in fact thoroughly guided by the observance of the rites, the teaching of the taboos, and, from the age of seven, by the first ritual tattooing that gave the child its rank. On this occasion one of his mother's brothers would give him some chickens. These birds were, together with rats, the only animals on the island, and they formed an extremely valuable and much appreciated gift.

It was odd how these fowls took on such great importance in Easter Island. As they were the only kind of meat, unless one counts the rats, they were so highly regarded that the men of earlier days erected strange buildings for them. The first explorers took them for burial-places, but they were in fact immense rectangles or ovals of heavy stones with roosting places in them. Every night the owners carefully put the birds inside and shut the entrances with big, perfectly-fitting stones. These *hare-moa* stood immediately next to the reed huts, and were continually watched.

Every day, too, we used to rediscover the remains of these deserted villages. There is one fascinating aspect that strikes the observer immediately, and that is the disproportion between the ahu with their now fallen statues on the one hand and the ruins of the houses, the hare-moa and the stone ovens on the other. Try to picture the impressive outline of these statues, dominating the village and perpetually gazing at it. With their backs turned to the sea, these giants look as though they had wanted to hold the men prisoner upon that rock at the world's end. It is a tremendous disproportion and once again it calls to mind the religious fervour that enabled these men to transcend themselves as they carved the great statues. Do we have here the panic syndrome of people who feel hopelessly imprisoned and escape wildly into a world of giants?

It is likely that these stone giants have had a fleeting life of no more than two hundred years; but they are still there, they who dominated the land of men and who now lie flat on their faces in the land of sheep—they are still there! Often, as we walked among the ruins, we were seized with dread at the sight of the huge motionless eye of a half-buried face. There are others that are still more frightening, lying on their backs with delicate hands crossed over a great belly, swollen like that of a corpse, lying there motionless, gazing at the sky that tirelessly sweeps the shadow of its clouds across them. And then again there are those that fell across one another as they came down, like those brothers in the wreck of Hiroshima.

There was one whose face we gazed at for hours on end. Nothing but the shadow of his body was left; his eye-sockets were filled with water and only his mouth was still delicately drawn, a mouth closed for ever, and beautiful, so very beautiful, eaten away by the salt of the sea.

And along the line of these statues were the huts. Five or six canoe-huts between fifty and seventy feet long, room for some hundred and fifty people: this was the village of the ahu, the village of peace, for here the statues were still standing.

Let us try to recapture the life of the village, as though the grass and totora roofs were still there, steaming in the first rays of the sun.

As soon as the village woke it sprang into life after the long cramped night in the dark huts. The children went off to swim and the men and women to their various tasks—some to work in the fields, some to go fishing and others to set about the building of a new hut.

The building of a hut called for the combined efforts of the whole group. In this case it was a great hut with a length of more than a hundred feet that was to be finished, but before the final stage months and months of work had been needed for the carrying and cutting of the fine stone slabs that made up the oval base. The slabs, carefully stood on edge, had previously been provided with a great many large holes, very hard to make with stone drills—and into these holes the men now set the framework branches of *ti* [an edible plant that has a fairly strong stalk] or sugar-cane which, bent like a boat's ribs, met on a slender ridge-pole. Others prepared the neatly-sewn totora matting that would act as a roof and that they would cover with a mixture of earth and grass. Following the shape cast by the shadow of the roof, the leader of the group laid big pebbles close-packed in crescent-shaped patterns. The hut had a doorway, a very small one, cut out of the totora in the middle.

When it was all finished it looked quite trifling at the foot of the statues. But these houses, shaped like upturned canoes, were very cleverly built, for without wood, there was no other possible way of erecting a hut that could withstand the terrible blasts of wind that so often hit the island. These huts, with their hull-like shape, gave the elements no hold.

Once the hut was finished and the stone pillows shaped, the mats and the stone bowls were carefully set out in the shade. The doorway had a stone slab on either side of it, and in front of it were placed two small stone or wooden statues.

When all these things were done, the hut was consecrated by the king.

Meanwhile some of the people had gone to work their plots of land—plots whose boundaries were very exactly drawn. The man would take his digging stick, and he would see to the watering and the growth of the plants that were, together with eggs, poultry and fish, his only source of food. He had a thorough knowledge of his land, and he was acquainted with forty-two kinds of yam and twenty of *taro*. With these, his sweet potatoes and bananas, he knew that he could feed his big undivided family.

Furthermore, his brother had gone off fishing that morning. As there were not many canoes and as they were used only for tunny-fishing he had gone alone, taking his net made of the fibres of the paper-mulberry, his precious stone fish-hook and a few others made of human bone. He had gone to fish among the rocks. If he could not catch any fish, he would at all events dive and catch crayfish, trepang and small shellfish. Sometimes he might take octopus too, or eels, and in those days the turtles still came ashore on Easter Island—a rare treat.

When he came home he would light a fire by twirling an upright stick in a wooden groove, spinning it fast between his flattened palms. Then the stones of the umu would have to be heated. Since there was so little wood he would use sugarcanes, grass roots or even banana trunks that had been dried for weeks. When the stones were thoroughly hot they were taken out so that the bottom of the oven could be lined with green banana leaves, upon which vegetables, fish and chicken were carefully spread, then came another layer of leaves, another of hot stones, and lastly earth and grass. As soon as the sun was past its height everything would be ready.

The little village was full of brisk activity. Here, for example, a man had been undergoing the ordeal of tattooing for some hours past. The tattooer, armed with a little bone comb, hammered the skin with quick strokes, following an exact pattern. When the pricking brought the blood to the surface he dusted it with a powder made of burnt ti root, which made the tattooing indelible. It seems that tattooing, a typical Polynesian custom, reached a high degree of beauty on Easter Island,

Shell of a large canoe-hut

Ground plan of a large canoe-hut

Plan of a large canoe-hut (approx 100 ft long). The base is made of finely worked stone slabs pierced with large holes. In these is set the framework of ti-branches or sugar-cane bent like a boat's ribs. The roof is made of totora matting covered with grass. The low, hull-like shape enables the hut to withstand gale-force winds the patterns sometimes covering the whole body. Unhappily we know very little about them, for the first Europeans did not trouble to reproduce them. The last tattooed man died well before we reached the island, so we could not recover anything in the way of a reliable record; and apart from a very few simple figures the only reproductions we know of are some patterns on tapa that are now in the Harvard Museum.

Everyone was tattooed according to rank. A large gathering must have been a very splendid, not to say forbidding sight, and it is easy to imagine the uneasiness with which the first Europeans gazed at these bands of warriors.

If we were to go from hut to hut in our village of former days, we should discover the rhythm of its life. Here was a man carving a *moaï-kavakava* [a particular type of statue—] from a piece of toromiro. He roughed out the shape of his little statue with a stone adze—hours and hours of work, for sometimes, when the wood was too hard, it had to be gently burnt. Then, using *matas* [a kind of stemmed arrow-head made of obsidian], he could begin the carving that would be the admiration of the village. For days on end he might be seen working patiently, for the obsidian blades were perpetually breaking and had to be replaced. When the statuette was finished he began the long task of polishing it, starting the process with little coral rasps. All the roughness had to vanish before the carving was completely polished and really beautiful. Then the grain had to be worked over for the wood to acquire a marble-like surface, and this was done with a *pure*, that beautiful shell women sometimes wear as an ornament. At the last moment the sculptor set in the eyes, using shark's vertebrae with a little piece of obsidian in the middle to give life to its expression. After months and years of smoke and respectful hands picking it up, the statue would take on a shining black patina that would make it invisible in the darkness of the hut.

On the stones outside the hut a woman was making the mahute tapa to be used for the wonderful cloak she would put on at night when there was dancing. With a mallet made of very hard wood she beat the bark laid on a smooth stone. The fibres, continally wetted, grew longer and longer and the cloth took on shape; then she cleverly sewed it all together with a needle worked out of human bone.

Next door another woman was plaiting the hats that she would exchange for cocks or sea-birds. She had already made several, and one of them was outstanding—a beautiful cap made of plaited reeds into which many hundreds of cocks' feathers had been worked with a great feeling for colour. Several feather head-dresses lay next to it: some were the tail-feathers of cocks gathered into positive bouquets; others, made of little white feathers, looked like flowery wreaths. Most striking of all was a strange hat of the kind the women particularly like to wear. It was made of totora reed and it had the shape of a crescent moon with its two horns elegantly turned up.

Close at hand there was a girl weaving baskets out of the strips obtained from the bark of banana-palms. Long ago it had been discovered that if the bark were washed it would yield quite strong fibres. This was just as well, for when Hotu-Matua's men reached Easter Island their pandanus seedlings and their little coconut palms had withered, and no one knew how they would be able to make baskets or hats without the fibre from these two plants.

When the woman with the cape had finished her sewing she would dye it with yellow powder made from the *curcuma,* and it would be as splendid as the sun itself. At nightfall, when there was a feast, the whole village would gather. The meal was always prepared in the umu, the stone oven. As has always happened throughout Polynesia, the feast would proceed according to a strict ceremonial which took account of the social rank of each person. The men ate first, waited on by the women, who could not take part in the meal; only when it was over might they and the children come and eat.

These banquets were opportunities for displaying one's wealth to the world in general and to guests from other tribes in particular, but sometimes they would give rise to bitter arguments and insults that might develop into open fighting. There were many occasions upon which they were held—marriage, death, the end of a tattooing, or the opening of a new meeting-hut— and they always ended with songs and dancing.

We know very little of the music and dances of former times; but from what various writers have gathered it would seem that the songs were performed in something of the same way as the Marquesan *rari,* the men and the women squatting in two parallel lines. There were particular names for all the songs, according to their category—religious, bawdy or romantic— and the songs were accompanied by waving hands and rhythmically swaying bodies.

Evening after evening during our stay on the island we recorded all the old songs that had survived, and we were struck by the polyphonic character of the beat and the modulation of the voices. As in the old *ute* of Raiatea, one higher voice would often dominate the song, leading it and giving it form.

We were able to find and record a very strange percussion instrument, one that seems, furthermore, to have been the only drum that existed in former times. It is in fact a stone drum, and its sound is as fascinating as that which comes out of the earth close to a volcano. The drum was made by digging a round pit rather more than two feet deep; then a gourd was set in the pit with a thin stone slab over it. A man, called the *vae,* stood on the slab and beat out the rhythm with one foot, modifying the drum's resonance as he chose. Most of the time the stone drum was accompanied not only by hand-clapping and the sound of conchs but also by a singular instrument that consisted of a human jaw-bone with its teeth still intact: this was used to beat time on a piece of wood. It gives a strange sound, an astonishing kind of rattle produced by the teeth as they play in their sockets: we managed to record it. There is no doubt that these two instruments, the only ones that are known, are of the most unexpected kind; and there is no doubt that the invention of the stone drum shows the absence of wood on the island. To make a sharkskin drum of the kind that used to be made in eastern Polynesia trees of a certain size are needed; but from an examination of the wooden sculpture of Matakiterani it seems quite certain that the island never possessed trees of a sufficient girth.

As for the dancing itself, we know very little apart from what the early travellers have to say about a dance that involved hopping on one foot. In spite of all our questions we could not find the meaning of this dance nor could we come by any knowledge of other movements. As happened everywhere, the missionaries at once forbade what they called the heathen dances, and they vanished, giving way to imported dances that were supposed to be more moral.

At night, when we were recording these last songs that bear witness to a world that has disappeared and when we listened to the deep surge of the voices, we could not but imagine what it must have been like in the days when the wind bore the sound of hundreds of singers chanting the love-song of the carvers of stone. What a sight it must have been, those groups of singers in their splendid feather head-dresses, as beautiful as the long tapa cloaks that hung from their bare shoulders, their bodies painted with the four holy colours, yellow, red, blue and black. I still remember the astonishing sensations we felt when in the silence of a cave we recorded the very pure sound of a woman's voice singing the Hiva song.

Every day we used to go into the maze of caverns, among the cliffs and shattered rocks, peering closely at the marks that life had left, watching our friends' expressions or those inherited reactions that sometimes shed so sudden and fierce a light upon the past. We would often ride out to explore the great lava field that starts at the feet of the seven moaï of Ahu A'Tiu and runs right down to the surf. There, among the lava-flows that hide the caves, lies the most extraordinary labyrinth of vast hollows, formed by the sunken gardens. We loved that name 'sunken gardens', for it retains all the poetry of an inhuman world.

These gardens were enormous lava bubbles, bubbles that had burst open, and in their recesses the wind and the passing centuries had deposited a layer of water-retaining humus fifteen to twenty feet deep, sometimes thirty and more. There the wind could not reach, and there, in former days, men planted the mahute, the banana-palms and what meagre vegetables they could wrest from that world of volcanic rock.

A wonderful garden, and when we reached it we discovered peace there, far from the wind that gives the island its forgotten music. This astonishing maze of sunken gardens runs more than half a mile, and from far off they can be detected by the faint haze of green that rises from them. A wonderful phenomenon, for all round their edges open the caves in which the people lived. Vast caverns, with defensive walls, narrow paved galleries, and then, guarded by a parapet, an underground lake, as precious as living crystal. Hundreds of men, women and children found shelter there, and they found water too, for one can die of thirst upon this island which possesses not the smallest stream. I still remember that splendid remark of one of my native friends when I told him about the rivers and waterfalls of Tahiti. He said simply: 'The country where the water does not die.'

Here on Easter Island the water does die: it vanishes into the lava, and sometimes it is to be found again, still alive, underground. Apart from the three lakes—the craters of the volcanoes—the island has few springs or pools, and when the wars of over-population broke out these places had to be defended to the death—death that explains the bones that are to be found in such plenty.

This island was acquainted with death under two of its aspects: there was the time of violent death, wars and epidemics in which the bodies were no longer buried but merely hidden in the deepest parts of the lava vaults; and then there was the time of peace, when men, not a great many of them, took possession of the island and raised the statues.

An Easter Islander was going to die, and his body was going to lie in the chambers of the ahu. His corpse, wrapped in a totora mat in the manner of the Guanches and the Indians of Lake Titicaca, would decay and dry on the little platform raised some yards away from the ahu. He would stay there month after month, exposed to the sun, the wind and the sea salt that would whiten his bones. A taboo would be upon him and fire would no longer be lit anywhere near by. His bones, religiously preserved, would rest close to the little village where he had lived, but his free soul would go to join *Te pô*, the night, where it would live happily so long as the people on earth made offerings to it. Otherwise it would come back in the form of an aku-aku.

A man kept his rank in death. If he had been a king or a priest, a warrior or a craftsman, poor or rich, that he remained for ever and ever.

When a man was dead his nearest relation, called 'the master of the corpse', was required to see to the proper observance of the rites that ruled eternity. While the songs of farewell were chanted the funeral feast was made ready in the umu. The master of the corpse was the only one who was not allowed to touch the food, for he too had become taboo.

Exactly the same ritual, with a few variations, is to be found in all the Polynesian islands. Tradition has conquered distance.

There has been a great deal of vulgar talk about the loose morals of the Easter Islanders. This was how most of the explorers looked upon it, though they never needed much urging to join in. Polynesia has become the theme of a kind of writing designed to titillate.

We know a certain amount about the sexual life of the islanders; but we also know that it was civilized sailors who brought them the syphilis from which many died.

We know that the women of the island, or certain women, gave themselves to men who came from far off because in Easter Island, as in all the others, there is an overwhelming dread of the results of inbreeding. It was already very strong at the time of the first Europeans; and after 1870, when there were no more than a hundred and eleven survivors on the island, it became a nightmare.

But we also know a very charming thing—the words a father used to address to his son when he married: 'Never make her suffer except by giving her babies.' We know that the women were respected and that their work was fairly shared. We know that adultery could be punished by death. We know that among the nobles marriage within the family was allowed between cousins three times removed. We know that couples could part freely but that the child's interests were protected. We know that sometimes a child might be betrothed very young but that once he had grown up he could refuse the marriage. We know that some kings were polygamous and that some very poor people were polyandrous. And lastly we know that the men of Easter Island sang love-songs, like men everywhere else in the world.

We heard wonderful love-stories. There was that of the Hangaroa girl who was persecuted to make her accept the embraces of a Chilean officer and who escaped into that part of the world which is forbidden to the natives. She made her way through the barbed wire at Hangaroa by night and remained hidden for more than a month, deep down in a cave, where the man she loved came in the darkness to bring her water in his cupped hands. We know this enchanting girl, and she had unimaginable dignity. Nearly two months hidden in one of those windswept holes. Two months almost without food and in the cold, for the love of another so-called savage.

And we recorded some love-songs, as lovely as those of Eluard.

That is what we learnt about the life of the island. Our scientific work was coming along well; we had already translated a fair number of legends; we had recovered certain words belonging to a strange, disturbing vocabulary; we had compared our investigations with those of the great scientist Alfred Métraux, who was certainly right in saying that the men of the island's prehistory were undoubtedly Polynesians, probably from eastern Polynesia, who made their voyage between the twelfth and thirteenth centuries. We were sure of that; but there were many clues that led us to think that at the very beginning this island may have had another destiny. And where this was concerned we were to set accepted logic firmly to one side.

We were uneasy, genuinely disturbed . . . and now it was time for us to go and set up our base-camp at the feet of the Rano-Raraku giants.

ELEVEN

The Sculptors of God

Our camp, protected by four tall eucalyptus trees, nestled in a stone-walled sheep-pen over against the perfect circle of the volcano-quarry. Week after week we were to see the moon rise over the lip of the crater and vanish with the coming beauty of the dawn. And every night we were to hear the song of the wind; indeed, there were times when it seemed to guide the course of our long conversations.

Once a week supplies came up from Hangaroa. As for water, we collected the rain and we washed in the dubious crater lake. My wife stayed at Hangaroa for her work, and we lived at the camp—three native companions, a woman for the cooking, my English friend Bob and myself.

We began our work at once. When we had very carefully noted all the visible remains in the crater it seemed to us that it would be interesting to attempt to make sense of the apparent disorder of the hundred and ninety-three statues that were still standing either side of the crater's lip, and to do this before we began our excavations in depth.

The standing statues were raised, roughly speaking, along an axis running from the north-west to the south-east, and every statue had a slightly different orientation. It appeared to us that the gaze of each was directed towards a given geographical point, or perhaps towards a star. We therefore set about making a very exact survey of their position, and what we obtained was a proliferation of divergent axes. This was an un-ending source of speculation. Did we have before us the plan, the projection of a sky-chart, as the name Mataki-terani—'eyes that gaze at the sky'—might lead one to suppose? It was not in our power to tell; but we were certain that these thirty-foot giants had not been placed on the slopes of this volcano without forethought.

We were convinced that these statues, whose bases had been so cut that they could be thrust into the ground, were different from those squared-off statues that had once dominated the great stone platforms. We knew that these had been carved to remain here, guard-ing the volcano. We were struck by the difference—obvious at first glance—between these and the ahu stat-ues. There was as much disparity in elegance and mean-ing as there is between a statue by Praxiteles and a dull late-Roman copy; and when Loti was here in 1870 he wrote, 'The statues? There are two kinds. To begin with there are those of the beaches, which have all been thrown down and broken—indeed there are some to be seen in the neighbourhood of this bay. And then there are the others, the terrifying ones, of a different period and a different spirit, that still stand a great way off, away on the other side of the island, at the far end of a wilderness where no one goes any more.'

We set down these radiating lines, these unequal axes, on a sheet of paper, and they fascinated us. One day, unable to bear it any longer, I made up my mind to go to Hangaroa, to speak to my wife about this piece of research and to find out whether old Veriveri could help us.

The reply came at once, and it astonished me. 'No, the statues have nothing to do with a star-chart. All the Rano-Raraku moaï are sacred, and each looks at a part of the world over which he has power and for which he is answerable; and that is why this land was called the Navel of the World. All the moaï that look towards the

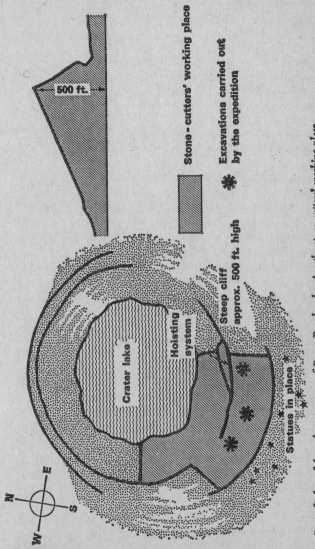

N W E S

500 ft.

Crater lake

Hoisting system

Steep cliff approx. 500 ft. high

Statues in place

Stone - cutters' working place

✳ Excavations carried out by the expedition

Ground-plan of the volcano-quarry of Rano-Raraku showing the stone-cutters' working place south are different. They hold the force of the Antarctic winds and they transmit all their powers to a huge red volcanic rock that marks the end of the triangle of the Pacific islands.'

Before us there lay quite another field of thought, one that we had no right to reject, since all earlier investigations and solutions had resulted in no more than verbal ambiguities or aku-aku tales. The natives' affection was to open certain doors for us—doors that have been hidden for a very long while. We were quite amazed, all the more so since I was getting frequent messages from my wife telling me of the translation of unusually disturbing records.

Now that this first puzzling obstacle was behind us, we could start digging and open our first site: but before that we had to make a scrupulous inspection of the vast quarry to understand the whole technique of the carving of the giants and, if possible, to acquire a solid body of knowledge that would guide us. We found the work fascinating, and in the evening, back at the camp, we were very much in harmony with our three Easter Island friends; as we talked, they told us things, searching back into the past just as we did, for they were as eager as we to know the history of their island. For them, as for all the people who were with my wife at Hangaroa, all this meant a nascent self-awareness, or rather, an awareness of renewed life.

Every day, as soon as the sun appeared over the Poike headland, we left the camp and hurried up the statue-pitted slopes of that wonderful volcano, so calm and grave that no words can give any picture of it. Here there seemed to linger the legend of a world that we certainly suspected but that we could not interpret. It has been written: 'All the travellers who have seen Rano-Raraku have been overwhelmed,' but it is an even more serious matter to write, after twenty years of research, that those who have seen the volcano of the statues are siezed with uneasiness like that which Pierre Loti speaks of in this wonderful passage: 'What race of man-

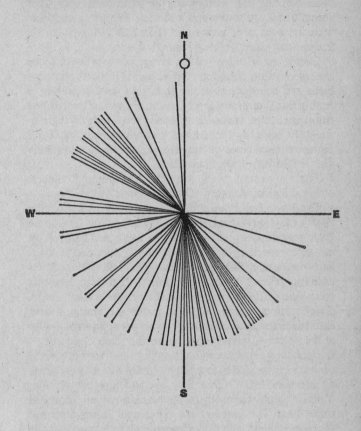

Diagram showing the directions in which the statues on Rano-Raraku look out. Tradition has it that 'each statue gazes at the part of the world for which it is responsible.'

kind supplied the pattern for these statues, with their noses turned up at the end and their thin lips thrust forward in a pout of scorn and derision? No eyes at all, nothing but deep hollows beneath the forehead, beneath the huge, noble ridges of the brow; yet they seem to be gazing out and thinking. On either side of their faces there are descending projections that may represent a head-dress like that worn by sphinxes or else protruding ears. Their size varies from about seventeen to twenty-six feet. Some of them have necklaces made of inlaid flint or sunken lines of tattooing. It seems most unlikely that the Maoris ever made them.

That is exactly what we felt; and perhaps that is where the great mystery of Matakiterani lies.

There are two hundred and seventy-six giants on the slopes of Rano-Raraku; and we now know that there are surely quite as many below the surface. The smallest measures ten feet, the largest seventy-two and a half; and that is what is so staggering. There they stand, motionless, present, sometimes violent in their splendour; and some of them are unlike the rest. They stand there, divided into two groups, some inside the crater, drawn towards the mirror of its pool, others overflowing the lip of the volcano, advancing towards the sea.

How long have they stood there? And why are some of them carved from a different stone, one unweathered by the wind? For there they are, unchanged by rain, wind or sand, while others are eaten away and covered with moss. The natives say, 'The ones lichen does not grow on are still alive.' And perhaps this is true, as it is for many objects that are called magical because they receive vibrations and retain them. Indeed, experience has shown that certain objects carved out of certain materials such as copper, dead wood and basalt are capable of acting as reservoirs of force.

With the exception of the exceedingly rare basalt statues, the nature of the stone makes it easy to distinguish between the two periods of sculpture. Moreover, the earlier sculptures are in a very much purer style. Almost all the raised statues at the foot of the volcano belong to the first period, and they were not meant to be taken to the island's ahu.

On either side of the lip of the volcano there are two vast open places where the stone was worked; but they must have been used at different epochs. The earlier was certainly that which lies on the other face. Here the great majority of the sculptures are very highly finished, whereas those on the crater side are decadent—much coarser: they are the work of another set of people altogether.

Every day as we moved about among this maze of prodigious images we were astonished at such audacity, such technical perfection. In order to waste no space the sculptors overlapped the statues, making use of every possible advantage in the rock—they set about them sideways, obliquely or even head downwards. Here in this lunar landscape they carved giants that belong to another world; the impression is shattering. Everything here is on the most tremendous scale, and it all gives rise to a strong feeling of distress, for everything seems to have stopped suddenly, in a single day, as though it had been hit by the blast of some enormous disaster. It is all quite inhuman.

Why did these men suddenly stop being the sculptors of God? What dreadful catastrophe struck them? Everything is there—the stone axes cut like huge Chellean picks, the statues halted in their progress—everything left exactly as it was. It is this which gives the sanctuary its unearthly feeling.

The present-day survivors do not know the answer: they tell a legend of such confused origins that one feels they never did know and that they are not the descendants of the last of the sculptors. They say that a witch who was deprived of her share when a crayfish was being eaten uttered this curse with all the strength of her mana: 'Moaï, be still for ever!"

But this is feeble; it rings so false as to be embarrassing. What is at stake here is something much more serious and disturbing. It must all have happened within a few days, for there are more than eighty statues still unfinished. There was no gradual slowing-down in the quarry. It was sudden death, just as it was for those dozens of giants who stopped in their progress along the track down from the volcano.

Was it a fratricidal war? Was it the madness of a king sent out of his mind by this vast project? Was it some natural phenomenon, such as a meteor that fell too near? Was it perhaps a terrible disease? Perhaps it was; for later we shall speak of strange carvings that seem to us to show a bizarre state of physical degeneration, something in the nature of the collapse of the cervical vertebrae.

A wonderful thing about this huge workshop is that all the operations are there to be seen, an open book. We know exactly how the figures were carved. Under the leadership of the head stone-cutter the team, which must have numbered about fifteen men, set to work on the chosen rock-face. With their hard stone picks—the rock for them came from the same quarry—they chipped away the stone along a line of holes a handsbreadth apart that the head man had prepared. This line defined the shape and the size of the work in hand. Sometimes the statue was carved on the flat of the rock, working downwards; sometimes it would be dug out of a positive cave. This was a prodigious labour, and it meant that they had to begin by opening two corridors two and a half to three feet wide and some five feet deep in order to get at their work. It was only when these trenches had been cut that the sculptors could start carving the moaï. The measurements were quite exact, and the head man always pierced these guide-holes. Sometimes, when they were cutting the stone away, the unfortunate workmen would come across a vein of scoria or intrusive trachyte that made it impossible to go on or that disfigured the work. In the quarry there are several statues apparently abandoned for this reason.

When the head, the ears and the body were finished the most critical piece of work began: this consisted of cutting out the back so as to be able to lift the whole from the rock. The sculptors, working on either side and following a concave plane, literally gnawed away the giant's back until the figure was held to the rock by nothing more than a great spine like the keel of a ship. The work that called for the greatest judgment was cracking this keel without breaking the statue.

We observed that generally speaking the sculptors tackled this ridge in different places, opening hollows into which they thrust large supporting stones. In this way the giant gradually came away from the matrix; and when at last it was entirely free it lay there on a bed of pebbles. The fine carving of the back of its neck and its back could only be finished when the moaï was raised at the foot of the cliff. It was then carefully polished with blocks of coral.

At that stage many remarkable carvings were carried out. They seem to me particularly important, because they are not to be seen on the decadent statues of the ahu.

In the first place there was a very beautiful necklace whose lines usually ran in zigzags, and in which, according to Pierre Loti, there were pieces of inlaid obsidian, though these we did not find. Now there is nothing Polynesian about this necklace; and the same applies to the tokens of tattooing that some writers have thought they could make out. We also often found remains of painting.

Secondly, at hip-level, there are three particularly unexpected marks. The first was a set of curved lines suggesting a rainbow, then came a perfect circle, and then a very odd incision shaped like a capital M.

Alfred Métraux says that these represent the bark girdle the men wore in former times. I do not think so. The one explanation that I had from a native seems sounder. He said, 'These show the elements of life: sun, moon and thunder.'

This is exceedingly interesting when one remembers that for the natives thunder represents what we call static electricity. Here, perhaps, we have a pointer to investigations of the most important kind.

TWELVE

How the Stone Giants were moved

One of the great problems that dominate Easter Island archeologically is the question of how the statues were moved to the ahu, some of which are miles from the quarry. This problem has never been solved, and even the work of the Norwegian expedition of 1956 brought no answer, for Heyerdahl's attempt at moving a moaï was in no way conclusive for the following reasons.

1 Because it was one of the smallest, and because it was dragged along by means of ropes over a very particular kind of ground that exists nowhere on the island except at Anakena—sandy ground without any rocks sticking out of it.

2 The biggest statues that were brought to the ahu attained a weight of twenty tons. If one remembers that the ground to be traversed is nothing but one vast field of fissured lava it is clear that there is no comparison between the problems involved. Many explanations have been given, some crazy and others unconvincing.

Some writers have suggested that a layer of sweet potatoes and yams was put under the statues—what a prodigious mess, stretching over miles and miles! Others have said that wooden rollers were used. But where would the unfortunate islanders have found the necessary timber? One has but to think of the stunted shoots of toro miro, all twisted by the wind, whose utmost girth is that of a man's thigh. Others have spoken of sledges.

To be sure, rope did exist, and we know its nature; it was tolerably strong, but even so one cannot possibly believe in these conjectures. There is another fact, even more suprising: the statues do not bear the least sign of a bump or a scratch; and when one considers the relative softness of this volcanic tufa it is clear that if the statues had been dragged on wooden rollers for miles they would bear the marks of it.

Reason naturally looks for logically satisfying evidence; but the most surprising thing is the unhesitating reply of all the natives—the statues were moved by mana. True or false, it is nevertheless very curious that the answer should always be the same. Our informants were categoric: only two men possessed mana. The people had to work hard to carve the moaï, but when they were finished the king provided the mana to move them. These things are lost, they told us; there is no mana left.

It is a mistake to smile at this kind of talk, for if there is no valid logical explanation, why reject a hypothesis that may turn out to be true? What if certain men at a certain period were able to make use of electro-magnetic or anti-gravitational forces? It is an extraordinary concept, but not more so than that of squashed yams. And on the sheer side of the volcano there is something wonderfully strange. Here statues were brought down over the top of dozens of others, without leaving any marks. Yet the movement of ten or twenty tons is by no means child's play.

One should not indulge in the kind of reasoning that says 'If such exceptional things existed then the civilization must have been exceptional too; and we know that it had only reached the neolithic age.' This is not really very sound, for in Africa, for example, we know of many striking abnormalities that nevertheless run constantly parallel to a society of the kind called stationary or regressive.

I find it hard to believe in what I have just set forth, but I cannot reject what may be a probability. After all, scarcely twenty years ago orthodox archeology held that the earliest date for the appearance of man could not go back beyond 100,000 BC; and since we are now very far from that reasonable but much too early dating, I am uneasy about all so-called possibilities. I am all the more uneasy because the natives say that everything died on Easter Island when mana left it, while at the same time I see the amazing evidence of a quite extraordinary past. It may be that para-psychology will find a sympathetic vibration in this island with its perturbed, confusing magnetism.

At this point I recall something else a native told me. He said that the statues moved standing upright, making half turns on their round bases. This really does give the impression of an electro-magnetic mechanism at work in a restricted field.

As for the setting up of the statues on the ahu, the Norweigian expedition intended to prove that this was possible by the use of logical means. True enough, it is possible; but, as I have said, the statue that was set up was one of the smallest, and cannot weight more than three tons. Besides, huge levers of straight wood were employed, the timber coming, I believe, from the eucalyptus trees that have grown in recent years in certain sheltered parts of the island. But formerly there were no trees.

One may also base a theory upon other cyclopean constructions in Polynesia which, as is well known, were set up by means of ramps. The only objection is that these monoliths were not pieces of sculpture that weighed twenty tons and that had to be handled in a completely different manner. And what about the red stone caps that were set in place more than thirty feet up, after the statue had been erected? We searched for traces of ramps that must have been at least a hundred yards long, but we searched in vain.

When one is confronted with a statue that measures seventy-two feet (the height of a seven-storey house) and that lies almost completed upon the Rano-Raraku cliff, then logic is silenced. Think of the head and neck twenty-three feet long and ten broad, the nose twelve feet long and the body forty-three. Fifty tons! Even now there are few cranes in the world that can lift such a mass. Yet there the statue is, framed in its two access-trenches, already three-quarters finished. And it was never made to stay there like a vast relief in the rock. It was made to be raised. The head sculptor knew what he was doing: he certainly intended to bring this giant to life.

In order to take away the famous statue called 'the Wavebreaker', which is only seven and a half feet high, more than five hundred men were needed, and they had winches and all the necessary material. With all her equipment and men, the French corvette *La Flore* could only manage to bring back one head, and much battered at that, now in the Musée de l'Homme. Easter Island had no trees, and there was little likelihood of producing a continual supply of fresh rope: with its five thousand inhabitants or thereabouts it was not Egypt, nor yet Tihuanaco, where some archeologists postulate an army of slaves.

So it is better either to say that the mystery remains unsolved or that the answer is on a completely different plane—that it is fantastic.

Before deciding upon the place for our excavation we wanted to make a few trial digs round the extraordinary squatting statue that the Norwegian expedition discovered. This piece of sculpture is undoubtedly one of the most interesting finds to be made on Easter Island, and it reflects great credit upon Heyerdahl.

Only a little of its head showed above ground: the whole statue was dug free, and its discovery called in question all the theories of the peopling of Easter Island. No one who is acquainted with the Polynesian style has the least doubt that the origin of this statue of a bearded man must be outside Polynesia; and I agree with Heyerdahl in considering it pre-Columbian. When

114

we found it we were very much struck by its resemblance to the famous statue of the god of the Olmecs. This was all the more fascinating for me since I had devoted a great deal of study to the Olmecs, 'the salt-water men', who were very probably responsible for the sudden artistic flowering of the Mayas. This statue continued to worry us. It was comparatively small, and it was oddly placed right over the volcano's great fault, so that it seemed to be directing this world of giants among whom it had been thrown. It had obviously had a separate, different history, and we longed to be able to discover other records of the same nature.

Alas, two weeks before we left we learnt of the possibility of other records existing, but we could not carry out the excavation because the governor had forbidden us to do so, although he would not agree to give us any official paper to that effect. We had probably not succeeded in maintaining the 'brother Latin' relations that he would have liked.

But for the benefit of those workers who may have the good fortune to stay on the island I will here set down the information that was given me by a friend, an Easter Islander. 'Buried at Rano-Raraku there are two moaï of women with round heads and fully carved bodies with legs. They lie near the moaï that has a ship cut on its chest and farther to the left of the fallen statue.' I believe this information is correct. We long for other workers to be able to dig out these valuable records.

When our trial digs were over we decided to open a huge excavation on the slope of the volcano, in order to find out whether there were other statues beneath the surface. Our first work was the digging away of the earth to expose a positive stairway of four statues that were in the process of being finished. We thus quickly acquired a sharply-defined, exact sampling of the stone-carvers' work.

Our second site was in an immense cutting twenty yards wide and sixty long. There had been a great deal of work in this man-made trench, and here, under a layer of earth and stone chippings, we dug out two magnificent thirty-three-foot statues. They were the biggest that had ever been unearthed; they were extraordinarily beautiful and the carving of the stone was wonderfully pure. They also had several details that we were unable to find on the other statues, which had been damaged by erosion. Apart from the line of the ears, in these statues the wings of the nose and the trace of the muscles in the upper lip were handled with striking delicacy and the utmost technical skill.

Here these first-period statues were completely white and very highly polished. But the most remarkable thing about them was their two hands joined at the height of their navel. Apart from anything else, the purity and elegance of these hands showed, without any possibility of doubt, the interesting feature that Stephen-Chauvet had already pointed out. They ended in prodigiously long, tapering nails—a most disturbing detail in Polynesian art. And all the statues that we subsequently discovered were of the same kind.

These long-nailed hands, which lie in the meditating posture, seem utterly out of keeping in this place when it is remembered that the practice of letting the nails grow existed only in China and among the initiated Incas, and that it symbolized knowledge, thought and exemption from manual labour.

We have only one piece of information about long nails on Easter Island. Certain children, to whom we shall refer again later, were shut up in caves so as to preserve the whiteness of their skin. They were initiated, and they were required to let their nails grow.

So it is likely that these first-period statues with the symbols on their backs and their hands ending in long nails (features that vanish or degenerate in the ahu statues) are not representations of deified persons but the image of the first god.

While we were working on this excavation our stratigraphy showed us a considerable deposit of burnt wood at a depth of two feet; at a pinch this may give us an approximate date for the stopping of the work on the statues. Tests we carried out following the slope made it certain that the whole cliff is carved with moaï, a fact that puts the entire archeology of the island on another footing.

But our most important site extended for over seventy-five yards in length and sixteen in depth. This proved to be an astounding excavation, and for us it was decisive.

The intitial skimming-off of three feet of earth laid bare the first traces of two exceedingly interesting moaï. To begin with we uncovered a bearded figure, carved head downwards and worked in the most masterly fashion. I shall always remember the awe that came over us as we took away the last layer of rubble covering the shoulder of this bearded giant. It was a marvel of pure sculpture. A shoulder by Praxiteles, in all the purity of very highly polished stone.

Our second wonder was the discovery of the most massive of all the statues, thirty-four feet long and sixteen wide, a monster in whose eye I could sleep. All around we discovered a positive jumble of figures. Under the overhang of the excavated grotto that dominated the whole site lay a giant whose body was covered with incised patterns. At his feet was a half-finished moaï, carved in decayed rock and abandoned. Lying against this moaï and overwhelming it with his huge belly came our giant, upon whose forehead lay a little statue six and a half feet long. After these, and thrusting them all back, came another figure, carved in profile. Then a medley of great figures, separated from one another by their working shafts, and then all at once, at their feet, a ten-foot gap into which we plunged and from which we extracted ton after ton of rubble eventually bringing to light an undamaged marvel some twenty feet long, a giant lying flat on a huge bed of rock and running on beneath the ground at a slight angle. This giant—his colour was white tinged with ochre—appeared in all his original perfection.

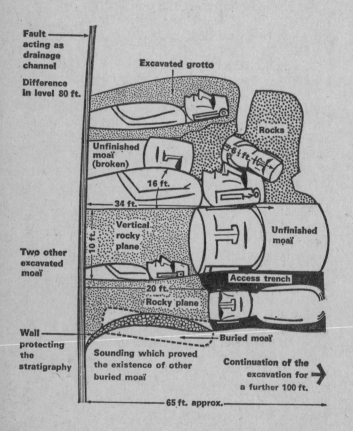

Fault acting as drainage channel

Difference in level 80 ft.

Excavated grotto

Rocks

Unfinished moaï (broken)

6 ft.

16 ft.

34 ft.

Vertical rocky plane

Unfinished moaï

10 ft.

Two other excavated moaï

Access trench

20 ft.

Rocky plane

Wall protecting the stratigraphy

Buried moaï

Sounding which proved the existence of other buried moaï

Continuation of the excavation for a further 100 ft.

65 ft. approx.

When the earth was completely removed and the stone had been washed by heavy rain and dried by the sun, this mass of statuary formed a splendid and a moving sight. Our native friends rode over to see our discoveries and our way of working, which they liked, for we wielded spade and pick side by side with our islanders. For us the sweat and weariness approximated to the tremendous labours of the sculptors of the giant gods. We were reliving a time that had no parallel of any kind.

Quite apart from the discovery of this jumble of statues, a ladder of life, as it were, all down the cliff, there was one thing that seemed to us particularly abnormal and worrying. How did it come about that these lower statues—and there were plenty more—were covered over with rubble and earth, while for two hundred feet and more above them there lay other figures, free from the rock and ready to leave their hollows? Either the men had begun by cutting into the cliff at the top and had brought the statues down the slope, in which case the lower statues were inexplicable. Or they had started at the bottom, in which case why had they not taken away the statues that we had just discovered—why was each not taken away as it was finished and ready to go?

A more thorough analysis showed us that all the statues carved at the top of the cliff—and this applied to the whole rim—were far less carefully made and above all were cut out of a distinctly poorer stone. They belonged to the second period.

This tended to strengthen our opinion: there had indeed been two periods, two migrations, and in between the quarry must have been abandoned for years and years. During this time erosion covered the first series of overlapping statues that began at the foot of the cliff. The second migration, seeing the standing giants, took over that splendid art, changing and debasing it. The newcomers built the ahu, and by a curious anomaly they set up these adopted gods on their platforms, in the Polynesian manner. But as we find throughout the course of history, whether it is Greece adopting the art of Egypt, Rome debasing Greek art, or Celtic art being submerged by what was exported from Rome, the art of the initiates had degenerated, like the ahu statues.

All this supported Heyerdahl's thesis, particularly his research upon the finest of the ahu, that of Vinapu. Here there had been two great periods of building and a third of destruction—the historical period. It was certainly during the second period that the statues were set up upon the altered ahu.

We were making steady progress and delighting in it, when disagreeable news reached me from Hangaroa. The season for bad weather was approaching, the Hangaroa anchorage was unsafe, and the men looking after our boat were worn out. I had to make a choice. There was only one possible answer—the ketch would have to go to Tahiti and come back to pick us up in six months' time. It was a very considerable voyage—more than six thousand miles there and back—and our two friends who had remained on board could not undertake it without the help of another sailor.

We were obliged to go and see the governor and set him the difficult problem of permitting an islander to leave his island. Everybody wanted to go. The governor was highly embarrassed, but he could not refuse to obey an international law. I had been waiting for my permit to dig for more than three months (it never came at all), yet curiously enough this business was dealt with in a week. Both I and the captain had to sign a singular document according to which we were wholly answerable for all the deeds of the islander we were going to take. He had no identity papers—the natives do not possess any on Easter Island—and he was henceforth in our care and charge, like a child. And this child was more than fifty years old!

The whole village was in a high state of excitement, for one of their number was going to see the long-dreamt-of Tahiti. The governor and even more the priest, who never ceased inveighing against the morals of Tahiti, did not share our unfortunate friends' delight.

The day before the ketch left I was summoned by the *Jefe militar gobernador de la Isla de Pascua*, who informed me that as he had had no reply from his government he was forced to forbid me to go on with my excavations, but that he would allow me (as one Latin to another) to finish the wall I wanted to put up to prevent the stratigraphy from being destroyed for ever.

The whole village was staggered: the doctor and many Chilean friends came to tell us how sorry they were. We felt wretched about it, for we knew that if only we could have taken a plane to Santiago everything would, in all probability, have been quite different, because of the Chileans' natural courtesy.

We were in an unfortunate position, far away on the most isolated island on earth and up against a little group of disagreeable men. Our presence was disturbing to the German priest and irritating to the governor and an asthmatic little jack-in-office who had suddenly set himself up as the representative of Chilean archeology. But we were foreigners and we had to bow to these rulers of the island of sheep. For six months we had to learn how to grin and bear it.

We had lifted a fascinating veil, but everything remained to be done. We had still to study the Poike plateau and the strange ditch of the Long-Ears, Orongo, and above all we had to see the famous treasures of the caves. The result was wonderful, for the people opened all doors to us, doors that had been closed to others.

Our boat left in the afternoon. How moving it was to see the whole village gather to watch her go and all the children come to admire the man who was about to fulfill the dream they all cherished—to live in freedom at Tahiti! That same evening we were offered the most touching proof of friendship. In the name of our native friends we were handed the famous manuscript that Thor Heyerdahl had so longed for. It is a time-yellowed book that contains, in addition to some remarkable texts, the translation of almost all the Rongo-Rongo signs into the Easter Island language; and the signs themselves are there, very carefully drawn.

When we looked thoroughly into this book, which was finished in 1936, we found that it was a copy of the work of the man who had given Miss Routledge her information in 1915. We possessed a remarkable document.

In their happiness the people soon let the news spread abroad; I was quickly and rudely summoned to be informed, as Heyerdahl had been, that we were forbidden to take anything old away with us. Faced with this kind of attitude and this kind of language I acquiesced and changed my way of living. When the people knew they were very much upset and wanted to give us everything: at all events they would show it to us.

For a few days I stayed with my wife to go through her work and even more to go with her on frequent visits to the old leper, whose despair I shall never forget. We both loved the sight of his happiness during our visits, which lasted for hours. My wife was going to look after the children of the islander who had gone off in our ketch—we had promised to take great care of them. We moved into his house, and it was one great family that gathered around us. Every evening twenty or thirty people would sit with us far into the night: but they were also twenty or thirty friends whose hearts were learning a different kind of beat.

The days passed and presently we had to hurry back to our sites by the volcano, to put everything in order well before the southern winter began. It was a sad, last task, carefully arranging our dig and cutting a few trial shafts that showed us seven more statues running on from those we had discovered. We were quite certain that the cliff was carved at a lower level.

We still had to film our work and take all the photographs—and, as we watched the sun, to gaze at the vastness of that unbounded landscape over which the statues dream. The sweeping gaze from these blind faces is strange; it broadens and narrows, opening and closing according to the rhythm of the sunlit hours. Perhaps that is where the high, magic beauty of these eyeless giants resides.

We shall never forget those hours of watching from the top of the cliff, for in the silence and the emptiness of that dead island we felt a wholly different vibration of life.

Before the winter rains began we carried out a further exploration of the Poike plateau, where a native friend had told us there were more strange statues. When dawn broke we would saddle our horses and gallop the few miles that lay between us and the towering Poike cliff. There we had a magnificent view, for on one side we were high above the huge Rano-Raraku crater at the moment when the sun touched the water of the lake that looks up at the sky, and on the other we gazed down on the immensity of the sea, tirelessly gnawing away at the cliff.

We wandered about this plateau for days, and in what is called 'the uninhabited land' we discovered a surprising number of villages of a completely different structure. Here, without any doubt, another kind of people had lived or taken refuge—perhaps the famous Long-Ears?

It was tragic: we should so much have liked to carry out extensive excavations, for these village remains have never been studied at all.

One day our friend led us to a very small ahu indeed; it was completely buried, but from this graveyard there emerged some remarkable statues. They were small, but the stone from which they were carved and their aspect were totally unlike the rest. The exceedingly hard stone was of the kind that was used to make *toki* in the old days, those splendid stone axes that oddly enough have the same name in Araucania and the Gambier islands. But apart from the size of these figures, the most striking thing was their expression—exceedingly harsh and most uncommonly authoritative. In our opinion these are the earliest of them all.

What kind of men were they who lived on the Poike plateau? Did they come from Polynesia or did they come from South America? Who can tell? The ground of this island will have to be dug deep to discover the true beginnings; but the great drama was certainly played out at Poike. It was here that the descendants of the first race lived: it was here that they took shelter. The axes and the stones used in building the huts we found were different; the villages were different; the rock-carvings and even that astonishing great head cut in the cliff were different.

Why do the two most remarkable caves look towards the east and why are they far out on the extremity of the Poike cliff? That was where the strangest of the rites was performed, where children of both sexes were shut up in the darkness so that their skins should be white and their hair and nails grow long, so that they should remain virgin and acquire another kind of knowledge: they were called the *Neru,* and there is a song that runs—

> Head coloured with the colours of the earth,
> Cave of the ancient Neru
> Cave of the Others!

We know so little apart from that rite and the last lines of the song with its 'cave of the Others!' But we do know that this custom existed in the Andes and at Mangareva too. What then? Other evidence must be found, other skulls: a study in comparative anthropology is called for. It is all waiting to be discovered, but to do so one would need to be able to live on the island for years, and to live there in freedom.

THIRTEEN

The Death of the Unknown Race: the Poike Dyke

The strange sloping Poike plateau ends in a singular cleft opposite Rano-Raraku; and this ditch or dyke has its legend. Many writers, Heyerdahl among them, have dealt with its history, drawing upon the legend of the extermination of the Long-Ears; others, including Métraux and the geologists, hold that this cleft is merely a natural fold caused by the meeting of two layers of lava.

What is certain is that this cleft, which runs for nearly two miles, completely cutting the Poike plateau off from the rest of the island, is something to make one think. Was it really dug out by men, or used by them? Before we give some of our own personal conclusions we must recount the story of the war to the death between the Hanau Eepe and the Hanau Momoko, a legend that calls for certain comments.

It runs: 'The island was ruled by the Hanau Eepe, the Long-Ears.[1] It was they who built the ahu. The Hanau Momoko, the men with short ears, worked for them. When the Long-Ears had had all the stones on the Poike plateau thrown into the sea they ordered the Hanau Momoko to do the same for the rest of the island, so that they could grow crops everywhere.'

Here a comment is in order: we can scarcely believe in

[1] I use the term Long-Ears on purpose, since that is how we were told the legend.

the possibility of the whole of the Poike plateau being entirely cleared of stones. It is far more likely that this came about naturally, for here the volcano did not burst forth but thrust up the ground, thus forming the peninsula.

'The Hanau Momoko refused, saying they needed the stones to cook their food and to make the taro grow better. Faced with this refusal, the Long-Ears withdrew to Poike and dug a huge ditch in case of attack, which they filled with branches, cane stalks and grass. The Hanau Momoko were warned by a woman of their own race who was married to a Long-Ears, and they determined to set upon the Long-Ears at a given signal. When they saw Moko Pingei weaving a basket they were to make their way into the Poike plateau by night, passing along the edge of the cliff. Then other Hanau Momoko would attack the ditch from the front. This is what happened. The Long-Ears set fire to the dyke, but they were suddenly attacked from behind, and only three managed to escape from the flames into which they were hurled. Pursued by the Hanau Momoko, these three survivors hid in a cave at Anakena. Two of them were killed with long obsidian-headed spears, but the last, feeling death near at hand, uttered a cry that echoed through and through the cave, "Orro, ororo!" He was spared and given the name of Ororoina. He married a Hanau Momoko woman and he had a great many children by her.'

There briefly, is the legend; and it leaves me, for my part, full of doubt. It has the ring of something made up from beginning to end. A fire stretching for two miles and all those Long-Ears flung into it? This theory of the dyke had to be verified once more. We excavated a considerable area to a depth of sixteen feet. We at once found that layer of red earth described by the Norwegian expedition, sandwiched between the rest for several yards, a few scraps of charred twig or rather of grass roots, but not the slightest vestige of a deliberate fire, of a furnace in which men might have died. Nothing.

Granted there had been a brush fire on the Poike peninsula—there had been several. All the grass and low
bushes had burnt—it happens still in the dry season.
Then in the course of years the movement of the rain-
washed soil brought all these remains into the natural
fault at the foot of the Poike plateau. It really seems to
us that Alfred Métraux was right. But what then? One
day a descendant of the Long-Ears told us something
quite different, something that we found particularly interesting. He said that the Hanau Momoko did rebel
against the Hanau Eepe, and for the reasons given; but
he went on, 'There were about a hundred Hanau Eepe
and they took refuge on Poike. There they were surrounded in battle and thrown from a cliff to the south of
the natural cleft, high over Hotu-Iti. They were mas-
sacred and roasted in an oven called *Ko te umu o te
Hanau Eepe*. Their land was burnt and there was a cannibal feast . . .' This tradition seems to us more credible;
but we have it only from a single source—though this
informant is one of the last initiates on the island.

One fact is certain, and we think it of the utmost interest. These Hanau Eepe were the sculptors in the
quarry, and it is likely that the work came to a sudden
stop at that date—around two and a half centuries ago.

We do not know where the men called the Hanau
Eepe, the Long-Ears, or more properly the Strong Men,
came from. But perhaps the legend of Anua-Motua's
voyage that we collected may provide the true explanation for the coming of this other race. Our informant said—and these details are interesting—'It was
not in Hotu-Matua's days that the Hanau Eepe came.'
The king of Easter Island, at the time of their appearance, was Tu'ukoiho.

An interesting point, for according to the royal genealogy in the book given to us when our ketch sailed, this
name appears as the fifth after Hotu-Matua, that is to
say, if we allow about twenty years to a generation, a
century after Hotu-Matua's arrival. Seeing that the

dates agree, it may be that the second migration took place at this period.

Our informant added, 'There were no women, only men: there were many of them and they lived at Poike.'

No women: that means there was necessarily a mixing of blood and hence the possibility of the two groups living and working together. Customs could be transferred, too: for example, the stretching of the ears, which was carried on long after all the Long-Ears except one had been destroyed.

Although we are forced to doubt some of our own conclusions we will try to set up a relative chronology that may perhaps allow us, as we go on, either to reject our conclusion or to hold it with greater conviction.

1 According to our genealogy, which runs from the coming of Hotu-Matua to the death of the little king Gregorio, some six centuries seem to have elapsed during this period. We are of the opinion that Hotu-Matua's men, coming from the outermost Marquesas, landed in about the twelfth century.

2 According to the genealogy of Tu'ukoiho, the second migration of the Hanau Eepe reached Matakiterani towards the end of the thirteenth century.

3 According to the genealogies of the Long-Ears' descendants who now live on the island, the massacre of the Long-Ears took place about 1760: this gives us a remarkable date, for in 1722 Roggeveen speaks of the statues as standing and in 1774 Cook mentions their partial destruction.

So it would seem that the Long-Ears worked and lived with Hotu-Matua's men for about three hundred and fifty years. From the point of view of the time needed for building up a necropolis of this kind we are therefore still within reasonable limits. If these approximate dates could be checked with certainty we should have a first chronology for Easter Island.

These dates embody one certain fact—the two migrations referred to were Polynesian. But they do not tell us whether there had been any earlier migration, nor who the men were who made Vinapu and the statues of the first period. It may be that they came from an entirely different direction.

The rain heralded the coming of the southern winter—a harsh season on Matakiterani. We had to stay on in our camp for a while, to see whether our sytem for draining the sites was adequate, and we lingered at Hotu-Iti, where the debris of the Tonga-Riki ahu lie—it had been one of the loveliest, with its fifteen statues, but it was entirely destroyed by the tidal wave that followed the Chilean earthquake of 1960.

This ahu has often been described by those who were lucky enough to see it when it merely had its statues overturned; all that can be seen now is its shattered remains. The tidal wave of 1960 ran six hundred yards inland, burying the Hotu-Iti plain deep in rubble. It is a painful sight; yet it makes one reflect, for here we have the most recent example of those violent movements of the earth's crust which we spoke of at the beginning of this book and which can alter the geography of certain islands. According to the natives, the coast-line was not markedly changed, but the strength of the three successive waves was such that the huge statues, the finest of the ahu moaï, were turned over and carried along for about a hundred yards. These moaï were between twenty-three and thirty feet long and their weight was in the nature of twenty to thirty tons. Some broke; others remained intact, lying on their backs with their immense eyes gazing at the sky.

We found this sight as extraordinary as the discovery of the moaï at the bottom of our excavation. But those had had their eyes opened, and their heads and bellies, overturned for some two hundred years, showed pale and livid in the sun. They were dead yet living, like ghosts issued from the great stone tombs; for some had been tumbled into the opened burial chambers and rose from them chipped and battered.

From the sea we had the most splendid view of a

giant lying on his back, his silhouette standing out upon the great shattered Rano-Raraku cliff; and as we looked at his corpse we could not but remember the curse addressed long ago to the Tonga-Riki statues—'One day the sea will take you back!'

There was a confused heap of carefully dressed and polished slabs, and they were worked from a stone that the natives said they knew although I had seen it anywhere on the island. One of the slabs was particularly remarkable: it measured about three feet across and sixteen long. With edges slightly bevelled to make it fit and hold perfectly, it was an architectural masterpiece. The whole construction must have been a glorious spectacle.

The great rains began, driving in on the furious, icy wind from the Antarctic. At night in our camp the tent began dancing ominously in the midst of its spider's web of guy ropes. The wind reached Force Ten and Eleven, and we had to raise the protecting wall quickly to be able to stay on in the camp another week or two. But there was something tragic and splendid about these nights, with the howling wind chasing the clouds, making its way into the mouths of the caves and leaving the darkness to the aku-aku. We were glad to know this aspect of the island, one that few expeditions had seen, for they only stayed during the fine weather. And we were glad that our boat had left, too, for the tremendous sea burst over the pointed lava rocks, and we could hear it roaring as we lay in our tent.

This island must be seen during the four or five months of the southern winter. It acquires a completely different aspect, turning into its own antipodes, the Shetlands. Its altered face makes one understand the terrible shock these Polynesians from the happy islands felt when they realized that they were the prisoners of these volcanoes for ever. It was then that we came to understand why they took refuge in the caves and even in the stifling atmosphere of those first canoe-houses.

They were sheltering from the cold, the rain, the loneliness and the recurring impression that the island was going to give way under the force of the waves.

Every evening, with the fire lit under the porch of the hut—lit with difficulty—we ate together and stayed on talking, feeling the strong presence of this world, and of course discussing secret caves. Sometimes, too, we set off by night to see certain caves that our native friends preferred to show us that way, for fear of being detected. Often the manager of the Fundo, the Chilean Navy's sheep-breeding sation, would come to see us late at night; he was one of the few civilians on the island, and the people were very fond of him. We were always pleased when we saw the headlights of his jeep bobbing hesitantly about the lava boulders, for like our native friends, we loved him dearly. He always brought us some bread from Hangaroa, or a letter from my wife, or something kind that he thought of himself. We all sat up together and then, when the headlights shone on the track again, the great starlit night appeared. We would go to sleep with the sound of the wind and the rain battering the tent.

During the daytime we went up to the volcano to look at our excavations; all the covering earth was being washed off, and for hours on end they lay there gleaming wet from the rain. When the fierce squalls came back it was a splendid sight to see the scintillating water cascading from one great figure to another. We never grew weary of living at the feet of these giants: we were spellbound by their beauty.

The excavations became more and more splendid; the huge heaps of dug-out earth settled and rounded like the roofs of canoe-huts, and grass prang up everywhere, outlining the impressive masses of sculptured rock. Making the most of the lulls between the storms, we threaded the maze of statues in every direction. Sometimes we would shelter for hours under the torso of a giant, letting the rain sweep down on this dead world; and then, when it stopped, seeing life come back into the giants' faces. Lying there with their eyes filled with water, they seemed to be gazing at the sky in tears, and up there the sun, in a single moment would utterly transform the colours of the remote, unforgettable landscape. They were a fascinating sight, these eyes filled with the purest water, suddenly stirred by the wind.

'Matakiterani!' said my friend Teao. The island was transfigured: it was as grave and beautiful as Brittany in wintertime.

The men's faces were pinched; they were cold. But they were not so cold as their children. For years the men had asked the governor, the *Jefe militar de la Isla de Pascua,* to sell them a little wool to make mattresses for them. They were always refused. Out of seven tons of wool a year there is nothing for the islanders; everything is for the Navy, which sells it on the London market.

Our sleeping-bags and blankets made our tent an abode of peace, and, happy and warm, we could get up in the night and set off 'to do the caves,' as we said.

FOURTEEN

The World beneath the Ground:
the Secret World

It was the first time we were going to see a hidden cave. There are thousands of caves on the island: they were used as shelters, dwellings and tombs. But they are not the same as the secret caves, whose entrances cannot be found.

The hidden cave that we were going to explore that evening lay in the plain of Hotu-Iti. It was not a dark night and there was no need for a torch; in half an hour's walk we were there. Very carefully, so as to break nothing and so as to leave no trace, a friend pushed aside the ferns, lightly scraped the ground and then paused. We stared into the night, disturbed by the thudding hoofs of a frightened horse. Nothing, apart from the wind. Then he gently raised one stone slab and then another, fitting very exactly over a paved entrance. A splendid corridor appeared: it was exceedingly narrow—just wide enough to admit a man—and it was edged with highly polished slabs. One of us stayed outside to keep watch. As soon as we were in we switched on our torches. It was a little grotto about thirty feet deep, but for the moment it was scarcely possible to stand upright in it.

On either side of the paved entrance there was a drystone wall fitting perfectly under the roof. At first sight there was nothing to be seen, for the cave had been filled with mud at the time of the Hotu-Iti tidal wave. We at once began an excavation that was to last for six days—or more exactly six nights. Since we could not throw the rubble outside we decided to begin at the far end, moving the earth towards the entrance. The layer of mud was not much over a foot deep, and working at the round end of the cave we soon reached the floor. Gradually an extraordinary hand-polished surface appeared, strangely divided by a central channel four inches wide and three deep into which ran a number of smaller channels, the whole vanishing at the farthest point where the arch and the floor met together. A most singular fact was that the channel was filled with *kiea,* that extraordinary red earth with which both men and women used to paint themselves but which was also used to treat wounds and to dress the freshly-cut umbilical cord.

The more we cleared the ground, the more clearly there appeared what looked like a polished marble floor. It shone in the light of our torches like a dew-covered leaf upon which the veining stood out, red with kiea.

And so, by a necessarily awkward series of manoeuvres, we cleared the whole cave, which had been formed by an immense bubble in the lava. What we had before us was either a hospital cave or a place of initiation. But this great quantity of kiea that had been brought here and then spread out puzzled us. We searched further, among the rubble in the uneven places in the walls, and it was there that we found a wonderful thing, an object with no parallel on Easter Island and one that will make certain research workers see why we hesitate to regard the island has having been peopled by Polynesians alone. It was an admirably carved basalt figure a foot high of a woman in childbirth, though unfortunately the head was missing. My friends all cried, 'This was the place where the women came to bear the children of the kings!' I cannot tell; but I am quite certain that what we were in was a kind of hospital which was probably used for lying-in. Moreover, we subsequently found a number of obsidian blades that must, judging by their very particular shapes, have been intended for surgery.

This was the first discovery of the kind recorded on Easter Island. But the most important and most unexpected aspect of it was the statue of the woman shown facing page 48. Regrettably we could not find her head, which might have given us a great deal of help in recognizing her style and provenance. Night after night we searched through the rubble. But in any case the break was very old and had the patina of the rest of the figure. The head had been broken off long ago. Where did that little statue come from?

Throughout this book we have been obliged to hesitate over certain conclusions, for if that figure were not unique to Easter Island, then the problem would be quite different. The same would have applied if we had unearthed any of the pottery that we repeatedly tried to find, for we remembered the words of Roggeveen, the first European, 'They use earthen pots, as we do, to prepare their food.' Slender clues of this kind might call everything in question once more.

This was the first forbidden cave we managed to see. What we discovered was another world, the realm beneath the ground. On our last night there everything was carefully shut up again and covered over with fern: the cave was to sleep in peace, perhaps for ever.

The rain fell more heavily and more often; the cold increased. Soon we should have to leave our camp. We still had a few days, and every morning we galloped up the Poike plateau, all shining with the rain, to reach the uninhabited land. There, when there had been a heavy fall, we would sometimes find *toki*—stone axes—or building-stones, as though they had been erected by fairies. We criss-crossed the plateau upon which, soaked and stupid, there wandered ten thousand sheep, taking fright at the sight of our horses and stampeding, bleating, into the everlasting desert that is their daily bread.

Tomorrow the manager's jeep would come from the Fundo to help us move our camp. We had one last day for living in this enormous waste—one day and two things to see. Our friends took us to see a canoe-house on a hillock facing La Pérouse Bay, a remarkable building whose immense stone foundations were carved all over. (These stones would well repay excavation and examination, for their carving seemed to me unusual). It was the only canoe-house of that size and kind that we saw anywhere on the island, and with such a situation and with foundations of such magnitude, it must have been one of the finest. In my mind's eye I still see the restrained, dignified line of that perpetually fresh architecture against the broken, fissured landscape.

We also made a last pilgrimage to the volcano. It was hard to leave those stone men, dumb for all eternity, and those which lay where we had brought them to light. The rain had ceased, and the cliff shone with countless inscrutable patterns: here and there puddles held the reflection of the moving faces of the stone men, and here and there in the sky the clouds gathered in anticipation of rain. I stood there, gazing at a giant's face pitted with holes as though he had some curious pox. One of our friends watched me silently examining these marks. 'Do you know what they mean, Francis?'

'No.'

'The ones who were tattooed on their faces with coloured spots were learned men who studied the sky.'

The sky was flecked with stars for our last night—a night of silence, only silence . . .

We struck camp at dawn; the rain began; we stood waiting for the jeep, as bemused as children waiting for the school bus. We were to go back by road, towards the village of men, but behind us, as though to hide that cliff of the gods, rode our friends, followed by a band of wild horses raising a cloud of the island's soil which is now no more than dust.

We halted at Vaitea, the Navy's farm.

There is a little water here, which is why the English company, when it owned the island, chose it for its sheep-breeding centre. Here quantities of eucalyptus-trees modified the landscape, lending it a certain gentleness, and there were flowers round the house of our Chilean friend of cherished memory. Much kindness, a short rest, and then we set off again for the poor little house at Hangaroa, where my wife was waiting for us.

The track, if I may call it one, wound its way among the rocks to the gate of the Hangaroa camp. We hooted and the gate-keeper hurried to undo the lock. We were whites, and we went through quickly—very quickly, for I was in a hurry to see again all these people whom I loved and whom the sun and the rain had given the same colour as 'the Indians.'

FIFTEEN

'Among Men

Coming back to what is called civilization, that is to say coming back to people with undernourished minds, is a disagreeable business. I was at once summoned to the *jefatura militar* to give notification of my working plans. '*Conforme, señor!* I just feel like being with my wife for a few days.'

'*Conforme!*'

A great deal must have happened to make this prime specimen of authority as excited as a general about to be shot.

And then old Pakarari's house—Pakarari, our sailor, our friend—it was in his poor little house that his children and relations gathered in the evening to talk to us or to listen to our tape-recorder, which taught them that jazz existed and that it was magnificent to live, magnificent to believe oneself free!

'What's happened?'

'Oh, nothing, Francis; nothing!'

'Yes it has. Tell me.'

'Oh, I was worn out with working and continually riding about for food, so I went to see the Señor Gobernador and asked him whether I could have beef and milk, like the Chileans. "Milk, impossible. Too little. Reserved for servicemen's children." ' (This was true. The native children on Easter Island have no milk—not even in 1964!) ' "As for the meat, you must come at six in the morning and put your name down: six and a half pounds per family a week." "But I have twenty to feed!" "Are they islanders? Only you are allowed it." It doesn't matter: we shall eat like the islanders.' This is absolutely true; but the few tourists who spend ten days in the year on Easter Island and the officials who stay to enjoy the South Sea girls do not know or do not choose to know. For who among these poor people would ever dare to tell them? And I now know that they have cause to be afraid to speak. Who would dare to say that for eleven months and twenty days of the year the gates of Hangaroa are closed and that once a month the islanders, who of course have no money, are given one free sheep between two people? But these sheep are sickly-looking creatures. The wool is shorn for the Navy, but the flesh that is eaten is slimy and does the children harm—there is chronic dysentery. And there is not a single veterinary surgeon on Easter Island for forty thousand sheep. Will any government ever think of these thousand survivors to whom we owe peace and respect? But who is concerned with the Island of Silence nowadays?

The reader must forgive this speech for the defence. It is a matter of honour, for without that, ethnology is dead science.

During the three and a half months that we were still to spend on the island we settled into an organized way of life, happy in the company of our friends and in the difficult work that we had to finish.

It had rained all night and the cisterns were full; we had been up all the time, repairing the gutters, which were made of old tin cans. Dawn was about to break when suddenly, shattering the village's calm, the cry echoed from hut to hut, 'Miro! Miro!'

It was the same cry that had once greeted Roggeveen. A ship! And on this island the cry conveys quite another feeling—life! life! That is indeed what it means here. The children climbed on to the roofs of the huts and seemed to be dancing there, while everyone called out to everyone else, for a ship always means happiness, the chance of bartering sculpture for clothes and the wonderful things that come from outside. It means men from a great way off who sometimes talk kindly, slowly.

The American minesweeper went by in the offing, looking for an anchorage. And everybody rode wildly down to the bay, two or three to a horse, the women and children grasping sacks with sculptures, carved sticks and necklaces that they might be able to barter and which might thus change their lives.

But we were happy too, for we should be able to talk another language for a few hours, and hear a few gags! The Hangaroa jetty was like a milling village fair. The Americans came ashore smiling, relaxed, and everyone rushed forward, surrounding them and trying to exchange things. The Americans wanted horses, and it was a wonderfully ludicrous sight to see all these tall, loose-limbed sailors whose legs almost touched the ground suddenly galloping away, losing their caps and packets of cigarettes which everybody ran to pick up. Okay! And all these poor islanders laughed and laughed and learnt to say Okay!

Very soon we found that she was an oceanographical survey ship and that she was carrying a remarkable team of scientists belonging to various disciplines. The governor forgot to introduce us, but they were quickly told of our presence and they came to pay a courtesy call. We were soon on the friendliest of terms, and as they found the problem intensely interesting we decided to go to the Long-Ears' dyke the next day and carry on with the trial digs.

As soon as they saw the lie of the land and as soon as we found a conglomerate of charred wood in the form of a faint, continuous stratum—as we did in two shafts some distance from one another—they agreed with us. There was no longer any doubt—and this was the opinion of a group of geologists—that what we had before us was evidence of natural or deliberate fires, spontaneous or otherwise, over the whole of the plateau, not merely in the dyke. Our friends took samples from the sometimes very sharply-defined stratigraphy in our two shafts. They were photographed and numbered, for subsequent study at the University of California.

On the way back we went to see our Rano-Raraku site, and I was able to give them many samples of ti-wood carbon that we had left as we cut down to one of the thirty-three-foot moaï.

The scientists stayed in the village for three days, and when I had explained the position of the unhappy islanders they continually brought them presents and cigarettes. The evening before the Americans left they asked me if I could tell them who were the best sculptors. We all agreed that the simplest thing would be for me to gather all the sculptors in one hut, together with their carvings. When the Americans asked me how they should pay I told them just to bring everything they had in the way of clothing, shoes, soap and cigarettes: they seemed quite amazed. At nightfall they came to Juan's hut; with his usual delicacy he had decorated the entrance and he had laid out tea and bananas. Everyone was delighted and our American friends were surprised and touched by it all. Then began a wild scramble, with everybody wanting to buy several carvings, everybody arguing, diving into his kitbag for heaps of jackets, trousers, shoes, lighters . . .

It was a marvellous spectacle in the lamplight, all these people trying on the coats and the shoes and roaring with laughter. Finally everything had vanished, and one American, who desperately wanted a carved stone head, simply undid his wristwatch and gave it to the sculptor: I shall never forget how the islander gazed at me with astonished eyes, not knowing what to say, like a child looking at his father before he presumes to accept. Everybody was happy and I was the happiest of all, because my islander friends had met these scientists, who were so full of right feeling and genuine kindliness for them. Alas, they left all too soon, and the gates of

Hangaroa closed behind them as usual after a ship has called. Silence, rain and oppression descended upon the island once more.

Every night in our hut we gathered all the old men who might still know scraps of the ancient songs. It was moving, delicate work. For hours we would watch the old men arguing, reminding one another of particular lines of the stone-cutters' song, recovering tradition as night followed night.

For more than a month these wonderful evenings awaited us when we returned from riding through the rain. We all sat there in the hut, listening to the gusts of wind that seemed to keep time with the rediscovered song. When the old men knew a song they taught it to the others, and then we recorded it.

The chanting rose, slow and solemn. No one liked to look at anyone else. They were all very shy, for sometimes no one understood the words of the too-ancient tongue. When we listened to the recording all the young people gathered in the hut, silent and uneasy. The music, the call of a forbidden era, brought with it a strange nostalgia, a dreaming; and sometimes this would prompt old Juan to talk of caves.

Late at night, when the wind-squalls rattled the corrugated iron on the frail beams, some would vanish into the darkness to go back to their distant huts, while others, rigid with cold, stayed sunk in reverie until dawn.

Thus, in the happiness of these evening gatherings, we gradually assembled the last traces of that music. In the end we had taped seven hours of recordings that have no parallel at all.

SIXTEEN

Orongo, the Divine Observatory

After the adventure of the night, dawn would find us curvetting on our spirited horses, eager to gallop at full speed up the slopes of Rano-Kao, there to go to work on the magical site of Orongo. On the huge ravined side of the volcano bands of wild horses, their manes flying, would watch our approach, and suddenly gallop off to fresh solitude, sending up spouts of red mud.

Below, the cold wind lapped the Orongo cliffs in a mist of beauty as incomparable as that of the flight of birds carved upon its rocks. Orongo is a name that belongs to the wind, and it rings with all the magic of that place, perched on the ridge of the biggest crater. On one side is the calm of a lake half-smothered beneath the matted totora; on the other, the sea perpetually enfolding the three islets in its embrace.

Bob and I used to stay there for hours, gazing at these rocks with the fascinating symbol of the birds' return carved upon them in scores of places. There they stand, set like the canines of a huge jaw that surrounds a slight, carved platform; and radiating starlike from this platform run the seven corridors that lead to the dark cells. The corridors and huts are tiny; men must have entered them bending and lived crouching in the silence and darkness. What were they used for, these seven stone recesses? Perhaps only seven bird-men were picked to watch for the choice of the god Make-Make. Perhaps, more mysteriously, the initiated came here through the frightening blasts of wild nights like these, to receive foreknowledge in the shape of dreams.

The Norwegian expedition thought they detected a solar observatory here. That would have been a splendid purpose for the place, but there is nothing either to support or destroy this theory. Who can tell whether Orongo can ever be understood by archeology alone?

When we were making our surveys and had to wait for a little brightness to go on with our filming we were struck by the enormous attraction of this place of prayer under the stars, and I often thought of the words that Loti wrote while on Easter Island: 'What is more, I am in the grip of that particular distress which is the oppression of islands and which no other island on earth can give so powerfully as this one.'

Orongo comes to an end on the eastern side in a lava-fall where the side of the volcano has fallen to the sea; in time the waves will eat through it and discover the mirror of its inner lake. To the west Orongo is surrounded by a collection of curious buried dwellings—there are just thirty-nine of them. They are megalithic buildings, like the Provençal shepherds' huts or the Sardinian *nuraghi*. Here the stones were laid beneath the surface while concentric rings of thin slabs were built up over them, forming a slightly rounded roof: these roofs are covered with earth and grass-grown. From a distance there is nothing to be seen, as though these dwellings of the bird-men had wished to respect the flow of the winds which bore the birds. Almost all the entrances of these dark cells open on to the three islets where the birds nested. The huts are all built according to the lie of the land, which slopes towards the sea: their walls are courses of stone laid horizontally, but on the inside they are lined with broad slabs set upright. In the old days some of them were magnificent, being painted or carved with Tangata-Manu or figures of Make-Make. These have almost all been taken away or stolen: we found only a few, and those in poor condition, particularly the painted ones, for most of the roofs have collapsed because of animals standing on them or, more sadly, because of the activities of the occasional tourists the Chilean Navy brings here.

These huts, almost all of which are oval, measure about seven yards in length and two in width: the ceiling is rarely higher than five feet four inches. It appears, however, that these buildings sank while at the same time their floors became covered with earth, and that formerly it was just possible to stand up in them.

Katherine Routledge says that these huts were formerly used to house those who attended the ceremonies at Orongo; and in front of one of them there is still to be seen the remains of a very large paved area which was no doubt used for the dancing.

The whole site needs to be cleared and above all taken care of; this would provide healthy exercise for the Chilean soldiers and it would have the merit of preserving artistic treasures that belong to the world. Instead, the site is being allowed to decay still further.

Considering the number of these huts and their size, it can be calculated that during the spring festivities some four hundred people might have lived here. What a sight it must have been—the tattooed men and the women in their wind-blown cloaks upon that dizzy ridge.

Often, when we went up to the volcano in the morning, little Atan-Atan went with us, riding bareback. It was charming to see this four-year-old skipping about among the carved rocks or vanishing into the narrow entrance of the huts. He was interested in everything, and we would hear him call us when he had found a new picture or an obsidian graver wedged between the stones. It was wonderful for us to see him laugh, happy in his freedom; for how many children did we know, and even adults, who had never passed through the gates of Hangaroa? When little Atan-Atan grows up I feel that he will no longer put up with the *Ausweis*[1] to leave the village.

While we were finishing our surveys on the Orongo site my wife went to see several caves that the natives would show only to her. Every evening she gave us a minutely-detailed description of them—there was that Poike cave, for example, with the whole of its interior dressed and polished, and niches cut in the stone, shaped like the objects they held. Although sometimes I was sad not to be able to see these treasures I could entirely understand the attitude of these Polynesians with regard to my wife, whose Rangiroa genealogy they knew.

One thing we know for sure, whatever others have written, is that *nobody* has ever gone into the real family caves, where there remain the treasures of a world that has otherwise been stripped of everything. No one has ever seen them. There are very few of these caves left, perhaps a dozen; the entrances of the others have been lost for ever, the last of the old people having preferred to die in silence rather than speak, for you can imagine the state of affairs if certain people on the island were to suspect the existence of a family cave. The wretched owner would never be able to protect his inheritance on an island where the law is not the same for everyone.

We had finished our work at Orongo and our plan was to go to the Motu Nui islet where the frigate-birds lived, and—even more important—to try to discover the remains of the astonishing ahu, known as Ahu-Ririki, built on the terrifying cliff that plunges from Orongo to the sea. Our idea was to cruise along the foot of this cliff in a friend's canoe and so reach the island. We had already been close to the cliff in our ketch, but now, in the dazzling brilliance after a storm, it soared up above our canoe like the astonishing frontier of a vanished world. A thousand feet sheer, a thousand feet dotted

[1] The *Ausweis* was the bitterly-resented permit the French had to carry during the German Occupation. (Trs.)

with eyes that are niches and caves which cannot now be reached. Yet in former days men, carriers of the magic egg, climbed right up that precipice; and upon it there was a stone platform, an ahu whose statues have been thrown into the sea and now lie there, their eyes peering through the seaweed.

How did men manage to build an ahu-moaï in a place where we could not even land from a canoe? In a place where no one can climb the mountain any more? What mana was capable of taking the statues there, a weight of many tons? Who? How? We are far from the theory of crushed yams and wooden rollers!

These statues perched six hundred feet up on this sheer wall must have been an awe-inspiring sight—mad as the eyes that watched Motu Nui, where the spell was played out.

Sometimes it seems that these islanders, who apparently had had only a heathen religion, were very close to God. Bob and I had rarely had so profound a sense of the spiritual quality of this island where our form of intelligence is perpetually called in question, for here logic no longer holds sway.

As our boat had been obliged to leave with our diving equipment on board we could not hope to carry out underwater investigations, but we shall always be sorry that we were unable to examine at close quarters these giants lying motionless on their coral beds.

The three islets rise out of the sea about a quarter of a mile from the cliff, and it was here that the men used to land for their long vigil, having swum across. They are strange little islands, and now they are almost uninhabited. Very few birds have ever come back since the rites stopped. The grass, flattened by the spray and the wind, is still there, but the birds are rarely to be seen. The natives say that there is still a secret cave there, and that there are tablets in it: its entrance must be hidden somewhere under those great tufts of grass. The 'watching caves' where the Tangata-Manu lived also remain, visited by the wind alone: in one of them there still lies a strange little moaï one foot four inches high. But what remains, and what time will never be able to efface, is the tragic beauty of the Orongo cliff, which rears up defying the waves and sees the dying of the sun.

The whole story of the Tangata-Manu was played out between the precipice and the islands, but it would have been pointless for us to attempt research that in existing conditions we could not carry through. It was better to leave the islet untouched: some other expedition may investigate it thoroughly in days to come.

Nevertheless there is one remarkable thing that lives on upon that scrap of land—the vegetation. The grass that grows here is particularly interesting for two reasons. First, there is its texture: it is long, yet it is thick and as harsh as lichen. Second, it is the old grass, the grass that once grew all over Easter Island, but which was destroyed by the sheep and by the sowing of special kinds for pasture. An attentive look shows that this grass is surprisingly springy and resistant. We slept on it—a natural mattress—that night, and when we got up we were astonished to see how briskly its crushed stems returned to their place.

As we talked about it with our native friends we came to think that with a vegetation of this kind the movement of the statues might have been easier in former times. It is a clue that should not be neglected.

SEVENTEEN

A Journey into the Unknown

We left this solitude undisturbed: instead, we spent cold, tranquil days in the crater of the immense Rano-Kao volcano. Our plan was to carry out a careful examination of its perfect circle, search all the caves we could, and try to find an extraordinary carved stone that we had been told about.

One cannot but gaze in wonder at the impressive calmness of the sublime, perfectly-shaped crater created by the outburst of Rano-Kao. It is here that the last three toro-miro trees live, sheltered from the animals and the wind—it is this shelter which is so surprising and gives these remote, savage screes their secret air. There they stand, the last witnesses of a people whose grave, sensitive art died because it had no new growth. We gazed at the precious trees, perched there among the vast splendour of the rocks. The natives watch over them silently as though they were children who might die at any moment. With these last seeds it would be possible to plant others all over the island and restore a little life; but there are the sheep . . .

'And then, you know, these natives are so bone-idle —they don't choose to sow! Look at my splendid carrots in the presbytery garden!'

Yes, indeed. Admirable logic.

The island's art degenerated because its material was no longer noble: it rotted like the wood from which the natives have to build their houses. And that island toro-miro was magnificent, a very particular wood: the tree grows elsewhere, in Polynesia and even in Chile, but the wood is not the same. Here it was a marble that drew its harsh nourishment from the wind and the lava of the volcanoes, and that was what gave that unexampled art its delicacy, elegance and hardness of line.

It takes hours of plodding across the screes to go right round the volcano. It is huge: close on two miles in circumference. There are times when the wind rushes and swirls round the great black hole of Haumaka, and then it is terrible, appalling. But when the smiling sun is reflected in its vast lake it is the home of deepest peace. There, in the caves around the edge, men dwelt in the magic of a circular world. There one may still hear the crowing of the wild cocks: and these were the caves that we were to explore, the shelters whose door the sun always touched at a given moment.

They were all beautiful. One alone, at least among those we visited, was splendid. This was on the north-eastern slope, half way up the crater wall. Its opening was a spacious antechamber, littered with obsidian chippings—a dwelling of light-filled tranquillity. On the surrounding walls there were some very fine heads of Make-Make; then the cave rose to a higher level, on to which there opened two handsome galleries that men had worked on. These led to two round chambers that still had a certain amount of light, and from them there mounted a narrow passage that dwindled away into tiny dark niches. Here, hollowed out by nature and improved by man, was a perfect dwelling for contemplation and for defence. A paradise taken from one of Le Corbusier's dreams. We ought to have carried out extensive excavations here, but since I was not given permission to do so I leave this work for archeologists who come after me. Not only are there a great many adapted caves all round the crater, but on the northern slope we discovered a positive terraced village. Imagine our surprise when we found several pieces of toro-miro among the foundations, untouched in spite of having lain more than a hundred years in the sun, the rain and the cold. It must have been a wonderful village, with its overhanging terraces some yards above the lake. Several hundred men lived there, no doubt; yet apart from these stones the only traces are the dwarfish fig-trees that cling to existence among the rock-falls.

This journey along the shore leads at last to an oasis of acacias—an imported tree. Here, according to our friends, there was a huge carved stone: and this was the object of our expedition. As we searched we saw high up before us, where a last convulsion had split the volcano's rim, an immense cataract of bougainvillea in flower. Its varied colours in among the grey of the lava gave the cliff an extraordinary charm—it might have been a scarf Balenciaga had offered to the mirror of the lake.

It was one of our friends who found the stone. It was a huge boulder, rounded and polished by erosion, and the lichen upon its surface hid carved forms and petroglyphs that aroused our liveliest curiosity.

Slowly we scraped away the moss, and there appeared a maze of lines whose meaning we could not make out. When the whole stone was clean we found that there were several figures, two of them being particularly remarkable. One was a kind of penguin with its body ending in a whale's tail, and the other was a head of a sort completely unknown on Easter Island, a bearded head, with its eyes divided up like those of an insect. From its top there branched a great pair of stag-like antlers. It was exactly like the picture of a shaman or one of those head-dresses used in magic by the Indians of the far north; and what we found particularly striking was the fact that this same form is to be seen both among the Siberian Tunguses and the few surviving Yaghans and Alacalufs of Tierra del Fuego. It is not impossible that there may have been some contact and that this figure may bear witness to the truth of Anua-Motua's legend and his reaching Cape Horn. The natives said, 'That is the insect-man.' I do not know; I can say nothing. But it may be that at some later time the photograph will shed a singular ray of light. At all events this figure was never drawn by a Polynesian: it belongs to another world, as do many of the things that make this island so very strange.

It was now time for us to leave Rano-Kao, Haumaka's great hole, in peace and carry on with our work in the neighbourhood of Hangaroa between the storms.

The farther we progressed in our research the more the people gave us in the way of information and records. We ought to have stayed two years.

At the foot of the slopes of Rano-Kao there lies an immense furrow round a knoll called Orito. This is the great quarry for the obsidian that revolutionized the island's stone-working industry and its art. There was nothing more beautiful, just after a shower, than the sight of these millions of fragments of every size shining in the sun. Obsidian is a black vitrified stone; it becomes translucent when it is worked into a thin blade, and it takes an extraordinary cutting edge.

The sudden appearance of this obsidian, lying in a huge, sharply-defined trail, makes one think of the braking, the coming to a halt, of a spacecraft. Who has ever examined all the possibilities underlying the formation of rock of this kind? Here again, a thorough investigation is called for. Unhappily our scintillometer had gone wrong, so we could not study the radio-activity of this particular obsidian, which seems to me quite unlike the rest. This furrow and its particular lie, extending for no more than half a mile with a width of about two hundred yards, haunted us, for it seemed completely out of the normal order of things. And above all there was that hitherto unrecorded point of impact, which lay on the axis of this line. It could be seen about a mile away, on the side of a hill, and it was emphasized by a different kind of vegetation. It formed a perfect circle, and it had the appearance of a place where something had landed with immense force.

As we searched hour after hour and day after day among the Dantesque rubble we found a great many roughed-out beginnings of mata and tools as well as large masses, coarsely dressed so as to be carried to the other end of the island and there worked into shape. Some writers have stated that the discovery of the working of obsidian was very recent. Our opinion is quite the contrary, for we found striking examples at many levels in the stratigraphy of the caves. There is no doubt that on Easter Island men made use of this extraordinary raw material from the earliest days of settlement.

The classical stone-working technique was employed, the mass being struck with a wooden or lava mallet and the last touches being given by flaking. The nature of the obsidian allowed a Mousterian delicacy, the rough shaping having a Chellean air. The tools we found, the blades, scrapers, arrowheads, knives and so on, were of a style peculiar to Easter Island, for they all possessed a stem. Specimens are still to be found by the thousand, but up to now they have been collected only on the surface. We had the unexpected good fortune to discover the very finest and perhaps the largest example. It was a wonderful find for people passionately concerned with archeology.

That morning I had to go and see our old friend Gabriel Veriveri and I was unable to accompany Bob, who had just found an unusually interesting cave: in it he had discovered a great many bone needles, and also large numbers of very fine mata associated with pieces of toro-miro, preserved in the mud of the floor. So on that particular morning Bob had gone off alone to sink a few shafts before coming to ask me to look at the details of the excavation that he had begun.

Just before lunch I heard the galloping of a horse. Bob, shining with sweat, jumped from the saddle outside our little house, and with a wink he gave me to understand that it had been a wonderful morning. Scarcely was he through the door before he showed me one of the finest prehistoric objects I had seen since the Lespugue Venus—he waved it under my nose. It was a *mata* of splendid size and in splendid condition. It was shaped like a semi-circular chopping-knife, and it measured eight and three-quarter inches long and eight across.

We were so delighted that we at once showed it to a great many of our friends, and the news spread quickly through the village. Imagine our surprise when two days later we saw the *Jefe Militar de la Isla de Pascua* and his asthmatic little friend appear, without having had the civility to give any notice of their visit, thrust their way through our door and walk deliberately into our house with the intention, as they said, of taking possession of the object that they had heard about. Without the least embarrassment these little temporary policemen were there to search the hut in which we were living.

What then? Nothing, of course. All that remained for us to do was to photograph the unique object and to go and put it back in its grave, which is by no means easy to find.

This was the first time since the days of the Occupation that I had seen the authorities of an allegedly civilized country behave in this fashion; for although it is obviously impossible to take objects of this kind out of a country, the possession of them during one's stay has never been forbidden.

The asthmatic gentleman in particular was in a high state of agitation, for from the point of view of his future career it would have been a great feather in his cap.

All in all, it was better like this, for we now knew how we ought to behave; and I may say that none of the objects that we subsequently found and duly photographed will ever be in danger of being seized in this fashion. There were two repetitions of this grossness before we left. Fortunately the great majority of the Chilean residents came to see me and to apologize. I have no need, of course, to speak of the politeness of the natives, who will never acknowledge this kind of civilization. At the time of his stay in 1956 Thor Heyerdahl experienced disappointments of the same nature.

Yet none of this vulgarity could be allowed to make us lose our time, and at dawn the next day we were in the saddle on our way to look at Mount Punapau. This was where the red stone for the cylinders that capped the statues was quarried. We rode gently along the little track that wound among the village huts. Angry dogs leapt out at the horses, which reared and set off in a sudden wild gallop. The sun was beginning to rise in a clear sky behind the ridge of Punapau, outlining the red stone mountain set in an undulating landscape that the rainy season had turned a brilliant green. Here and there we saw handsome clumps of the tree the Easter Islanders call miro-Tahiti, for it was brought here by the French, as were most of the edible animals and plants. It is an extraordinary little tree, and it has adapted itself to this stony soil, in which it grows with a most surprising vigour. The landscape of Hangaroa will be entirely changed in ten years' time, and this is the wood with which the natives will be able to build their houses and their canoes—when they are allowed to do so—and above all carve their curios, which constitute virtually their only meagre source of income. Unhappily the tree can grow only inside the camp, where it is protected from the sheep.

Rearing and shying among the deep runnels that the heavy rain had scored in the sides of Punapau, our horses climbed up and up; and that morning, as we rose, we found a particularly gentle landscape. Nothing was to be heard but the deep-drawn breath of our horses: nature stood motionless and silent.

When the traveller reaches the Punapau ridge a path lined by a score of splendid red cap-stones suddenly comes into view. He has but to follow it to reach the quarry, which opens before him like a fiery blaze. At the bottom of it there still lie a number of unfinished

155

cylinders. Here too the work stopped suddenly, as it did at Rano-Raraku.

The walls of the quarry are hollowed out in the form of a crater; they are very steep, and here again it must have been an enormous labour not only to win the stone but also to get the cylinder out of the pit. It is a strange phenomenon, and one that is to be seen throughout the island—at no time has work ever chosen to acknowledge a human scale.

As we searched about in the bottom of the quarry we had the good luck to come across two basalt axes of a kind very unlike those of Rano-Raraku. They were comparatively flat and their edges were rounded. Of course the material here is of a different nature, being a conglomerate of coarse scoriae, and it is easier to work.

Leaving the quarry and following the cap-lined path, one comes to a kind of marsh, which dries out when the rains have stopped. Round about it are some thirty cylinders ready to be taken away. Almost all of them are carved with petroglyphs and almost all are huge, their diameters ranging from six to eight feet, with a height of about five. Titanic headpieces. How were these caps moved several miles across country to the ahu? Some authors, leaving the wooden sledges to one side, have gone so far as to say that they must have been rolled. As though such a thing were possible in this wildly broken countryside! For their part the natives say, just as they do of the Rano-Raraku statues, 'They were moved by mana.'

About sixty in the whole island reached their destination—the heads of the statues; and they are still to be found, scattered and broken at the feet of the prostrate giants. The cylinders at the quarry are still whole, and on one end they have a slight rise, while the other face is hollowed out to fit on to the huge flat heads. These hollows are astonishingly large—there is plenty of room to sleep there or to take shelter from the rain.

But there is one sadly striking thing about the place —an enormous white number painted on the cylinders, as there is upon the statues throughout the island. During his thirty years on Easter Island the German priest has spent his spare time painting them on, daubing them anywhere, on the statues' noses, foreheads or bellies, and on the cylinders—no doubt for fear of their being taken away. These registration marks stand out as the most glaring piece of insultingly bad taste. It is absolutely incomprehensible that such indecencies should be allowed upon works of art of unparalleled beauty. This king of the island is much attached to *order*—a very odd word on the Island of Silence.

From the hill above Punapau there is an immense view stretching as far as Poike, misty in the sea-spray. We had been filming for some days, and now that the great rains had cleared the sky we were once more going to see all the wonderful things we had discovered during the past months. We had to travel across the sides of these enormous volcanic upheavals and reach the Ahu A'Tiu, where we were to make a survey at sunset and above all photograph that unique group of seven standing statues. The sanctuary stands in a strangely remote position in the middle of a great depression dominated by the Aroi hills, and the statues all face the sea—an orientation that has no parallel. When the sun sets, lighting them from the front, the sky behind turns black, so heavily is it laden with the clouds that always cling to the island's highest peak. That evening it was exceptionally striking, for rain was falling on the volcano and we were able to take a huge rainbow that rose from the mountainside and came right down in the midst of the statues. In the last moments of sunlight the seven figures seem to relive some moving experience, for as they stand there in the general glow the last rays sweep their motionless bodies, and for a few moments their shadow-hidden eyes open wide.

They are all looking towards Hiva, these seven statues that are thought to be the deified images of the seven first Maori explorers; and the natives say that twice a year they are particularly meaningful—in June and September, on the day and the hour when the sun stands still before its backward swing.

Between these seven watching faces and the infinity of the sea there stretches the lava plain, hollowed out by its great sunken gardens and branching caves. That is where men lived, and their faces were turned towards the land, towards Ahu A'Tiu. Amid all the tragic beauty of the island there is no doubt at all that this is the place where, at sunset, one has the most extraordinary intimation of a reality beyond our ken. This piece of another world seems to have broken off from the stars or from those lunar mountains that the Rano-Aroi crater resembles so frighteningly.

Very soon the night fell over this enormous beauty of violet lava, and very soon too we had to get back to our hut. At full gallop the horses raced along the faint track over the lava; sometimes it echoed beneath their hoofs, frightening them, and then again it muffled the sound once more. This sudden hollow resonance from a vault or tunnel makes a most uncommon, violent impression. Here the network of caves works its way under the ground like the arteries in living flesh, and sometimes the crust of lava is no more than a yard or two thick. That hollow echo from the tunnels in the lava gives one a vivid awareness of the appalling experience of the men who died there of starvation or terror.

It was wonderful back in the hut, with the light, the smiling children and the coming of our friend Juan, who brought me a delicate carving of a *moko*, a man-lizard. The whole of the art of the Matakiterani figurines is anthropomorphic—a very strange thing to find here, for this kind of totemism is by no means typically Polynesian. There are bird-men, lizard-men, fish-men *(Tangata-Ika)*.

We still know a little about this interchange between man and animal. We know, for example, that in former days some women used to have a little tame lizard living in their hair, which in some degree represented their mana. But we shall never know the delicacy or the deepest springs of this kind of contact between man and nature. The whole great pagan tradition has been shattered, like those red stone crowns.

Late that night a native friend came and knocked at the door of my hut. He wanted to talk to my wife, to her alone; but afterwards she could repeat his words to me. Bob and I, who were finishing the greasing of our saddles, went for a walk along the edge of the reefs. They were magnificent that night, brilliantly outlined by the gleam of a crescent moon. Some way off we saw torches. It was fishermen after crayfish, fascinating them with the glare. It was a spectacle worthy of the Bolshoi, these men quickly, nimbly, leaping from rock to rock, with their torches suddenly lighting up the great clefts where the surf died away. Silently they slipped under the overhang of the underwater caves. We could hear the tremendous crash of the surf as it broke among the shattered lava.

What a marvellous sight it must have been in earlier days—tattooed and painted men, the violently contrasting light and darkness, forms suddenly appearing in the uncertain glare of the sugar-cane torches. In this island everything takes on another dimension, and sometimes one can understand that in this place men might spiritually surpass themselves and achieve a transcendant art, something far beyond ordinary experience. Here the statues' gigantism represented the natural scale.

Bob and I could not tear our eyes away: we stood there lost in thought, gazing at these fire-dancers as they leapt upon rocks suddenly covered by the surf, or slipped into underwater caves which let the fleeting gleam of the torches shine through their winding clefts. In those lava bubbles perpetually lapped and uncovered by the sea, the orange and violet crayfish were dazzled and allowed themselves to be seen and caught.

On the headlands the wild horses took fright at the moving light and they set off to find peace in the darkness. Far away the governor was snoring; but the island dreamed.

The men were cold, for a gusty wind had sprung up. We all went back to the stone hut together, our hands full of crayfish which, as they struggled, gave out a strange noise, a wonderfully strange noise in that silence.

EIGHTEEN

The Legacy of Silence

In the hut my wife and our friend were still talking. Bob and I smoked outside, impatiently. An hour later the man left, going quickly through the night. He would never speak to me, because secrets are not to be handed on directly: it is necessary to have that chain of responsibility, that double transmission—a symbol familiar to my wife, because she thinks in the speech of the men of silence.

The man had come to talk about the sculptured cave, the one which harbours the last secret of those who were called the Long-Ears, a secret which says, 'They were the first before the first.'

For a long while he spoke of the hidden cave on the top of Rano-Aroi. He said: 'No one has ever seen a sacred cave and no one ever will—those who have written told lies and we know it. Yes, it is quite true: we made many forgeries, and the fair-haired archeologists came and photographed them in certain caves. Yes, it is true; because it was better for us that way—that way the quietness could remain.' But he also said, 'I can talk to you, and I am going to tell you about the cave my grandfather bequeathed to me, leaving my father out because he talked too much to the white men who occupied the island. And there my grandfather said to me, "Nobody can ever come in: but if you know, if you feel that you can, you may speak about this world. If you

161

wish you may give some of the things—give, never sell, for they are still charged with power. But you must never allow anyone to pass through the door." The cave is high up on the volcano, but no one can tell where, because its entrance is hidden under earth and grass. Sometimes I go there at night and I stay up there, attending to the moaï-kavakava. By the door there are two corpses on either side; on the left a toro-miro-moaï-kavakava; then two Make-Make faces; two well-polished axes; two fish-hooks. In the middle is the *moenga* tied in three places, and inside it there is a tablet; one stone lizard; two paddles for dancing; on the right, four stone fishhooks; two makoi tablets, much rotted; a stone statue, a stone axe, two child corpses; and above them, carved on the wall, a Hanau Eepe head; a length of tapa; a gourd of *kiea*. On the ground, ten toes; a stone tablet, a stone rei-miro and another made of wood; two stone axes and a very fine obsidian spearhead with its shaft; some mata and a badly-carved Make-Make.'

This is an astonishing account, when one reflects that this cave still contains four tablets inscribed with ideographs, whereas only about twenty are known in the whole world. We were to see these objects, but we knew that we should never make our way into the sanctuary. I may observe that sometimes it is terribly hard to master oneself and to silence a habit of mind to which the forbidden is wholly foreign. Above all, I was desperately eager to see that Hanau Eepe head carved in the rock. It would be a clue of the very first importance. Alas, our friend only drew it for us—though even the drawing was profoundly disturbing.

The objects that we were going to see were only the outer expression of things of the spirit. The spirit gave them this significance and charged them with power. Let me explain: whatever the religion or form of thought, even the most erotic, any object that has been submitted to human vows, actions, or desires remains charged with psychic forces that can, as we know, be transmitted and that are capable of giving out rays. Any object, that is, except those that have been made out of substances that have been essentially transformed. Symbols possess a frightening power of vital activation that the men of the island have never forgotten.

In this connection there are several disturbing, fundamental problems.

1 According to the natives, some of the things kept in the caves were not made by their ancestors, that is to say not made by Polynesians.

2 For the natives these objects are still a block, a source of deep concern that the Catholic religion has been unable to exorcize from the island.

3 All the sculpture is anthropomorphic. This osmosis between man and the primordial animals gives a glimpse of a strange knowledge, one that is not Polynesian.

It seems to me that this form of expression is of the very greatest interest. On Easter Island we have, for example, representations of the fish that is called the *patuki*. Now this somewhat frog-like creature is a legged fish that has marked analogies with the coelacanth; but far more unexpected is the tradition that says that man descended from this fish aften ten changes brought about by alterations in the climate and thence in his food, and by man-like reactions.

Ten mutations, ten changes of climate: these are exact statements that cannot fail to astonish. Everything is like this. There were bird-men, whale-men, and lizard-men who were curiously like crocodile-men. Now these men osmotically coupled with primitive forms of life show the impact of a completely different kind of knowledge.

Between symbolism and totemism yawns the chasm of an entirely different concept. These objects are so highly symbolic that the survivors of today are conscious of it and are afraid of them; nevertheless, they try to reproduce them.

All these exactly-formed shapes, carved with the highest artistic skill, are in the waiting and meditating

163

posture. Here this art in its precision becomes surrealistic and not magic—it is an art that has taken on flesh.

The psychic condition of these objects is quite unlike that of the present-day islanders, who are afraid of them but who show their respect by hiding them. They are the work of another race, and they are not Polynesian. It is odd that no investigator should have detected this marked difference of style.

NINETEEN

The Art of the Others

Apart from the huge statues, Easter Island has a singularly interesting form of sculpture—these wooden carvings that are called moaï-kavakava and represent a fleshless, or rather a shrunken and diminished man.

The main features of this sculpture—the emaciation, the goitre, the wen—calls for the closest attention, for quite apart from the perfection of its style, it displays an aberrant character. The goitre and the wen are pathological symptoms arising from specific living conditions that should be looked into and that hold the key not only to the morphology of this earlier race but also to the geological aspect of the island.

Goitre is a condition frequently observed among people who are either degenerate or who have some mineral deficiency. It might have appeared on Easter Island either as a consequence of unavoidable inbreeding, or, even more likely, as a result of the excessive purification of the water which is filtered through the porous volcanic rock.

Dr. Stephen-Chauvet has made a remarkable study of this problem on Easter Island, and his view is that the deformity is caused by an excess of salt in the water allied to a high degree of dehydration. We know that the problem of water was and is of the first importance here, and many travellers saw the islanders drink sea-water near the cliffs. From this it has been assumed that through drinking sea-water they absorbed an excess of salt. It does not seem a justifiable assumption, for we have tried drinking the sea-water close to the cliffs and in fact it is fresh or only slightly brackish, for it seeps out at the foot of the lava-flows. But what is far more important is that their precarious way of life and their dietary deficiencies brought about disturbances in the endocrine and pituitary glands—disturbances whose consequences are well-known. The obvious thinness, on the other hand, appears to have been caused by a chronic dysentery that is still prevalent today.

These morphological characteristics are conclusive facts capable of explaining the particular and unique character of this sculpture; but it is none the less surprising that if this physical condition lasted for centuries, it should so have inspired the carvers as to fix this as the archetype for representations of the human body.

It is permissible to wonder whether Easter Island may not have been affected by the disastrous irradiation of a world affected by entirely extraneous forces. Faced with certain striking geological mysteries upon the island, we cannot dismiss the possibility of some extra-terrestrial contacts suddenly irradiating the island, leaving anguish for ever imprinted in the human mind, together with the obligation to make votive representations of that period. Quite apart from the physical appearance of these moaï-kavakava, with their hooked noses and their terrible grin, the collapse of the cervical vertebrae and the mark of a break between the lumbar and the dorsal vertebrae are serious indications of the possibility of very strong irradiation.

A small number of these moaï-kavakava figures exists in museums and in certain private collections. They were never numerous, and the few that are still on the island are carefully hidden away in two caves.

The early travellers reported an interesting fact: they said that the islanders willingly parted with these fig-

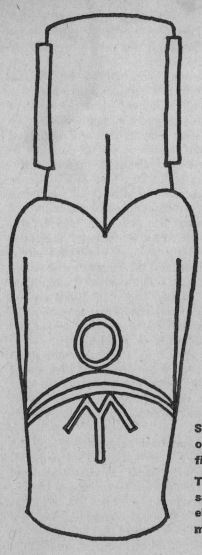

Symbols engraved
on the back of
first-period statues

Traditionally, these are
said to represent the
elements of life - sun,
moon and thunder

ures, which did not seem to belong to them. At present the natives speak of them with fear, as though they were something alien to them and they were aware only of the figures' danger and power.

One has a distinct impression that this art does not belong to them and that it represents another race. There is nothing Polynesian either in the facial aspect of the figures or in the way the body is handled. The explanation that the present-day natives give of the origin of this sculpture is curious, and like many of the other island legends it seems to have been made up from beginning to end. According to the tale, King Tu'ukoiho saw two spirits lying asleep as he went by the hill of Punapau. He was startled by their appearance and he at once carved likenesses of them. It is possible to interpret this sudden view of the spirits in a great many ways. But one thing remains and I find it most significant—these spirits were terribly real, and the king's representation of them had nothing magic about it. It was the representation of fact, not of imagination. The details are too precise, too deliberate. The king's dream may be nothing other than the likeness of the survivors of the first race that dwelt upon this little scrap of land.

The Easter Island art that consists of the stone giants of the first period of these toro-miro figures is an art of an extraordinary quality and one that suddenly perished at its highest point of perfection. As at Tihuanaco everything was there, set up and ready, and everything came to an abrupt halt.

It may be argued that since these wooden objects still exist the art is recent. We are not of this opinion, for the wooden figurines of the Egyptians have lasted until our time, and the Easter Island toro-miro wood is of outstanding quality: furthermore, since there are no insects whatever, anything made of wood may be preserved for hundreds of years in the dry caves. The texture of the wood might almost be said to be that of stone already, and on the island it was always cut at the time of the full moon—that is to say, when it was devitalized.

These figures, carved in so scarce a material, were worked with consummate art.

When the first European sailors appeared, Easter Island had little more than five thousand inhabitants, all of them Polynesians; it is therefore reasonable to suppose that this art arose among a different people and that it had been borrowed and debased. The decline is glaringly obvious. When the islanders had given away or bartered the genuine carvings they owned, they set about making bloodless uninventive copies, which they have sold from that time until ours to the few ships that call in. It is striking to note that all the morphological features of the moaï-kavakava were left out in the earliest copies, which date from the end of the nineteenth century. The modern art of the island has merely retained the apparently grotesque aspects of a symbol whose meaning has been lost.

Since it is now no longer possible to speak of any pure race of Easter Islanders it is no longer possible to speak of an art. Who, then, were the people who first lived on that island at the world's end? In the present state of knowledge we cannot make a positive reply; but it seems to us probable that this first race may have been connected either with the people of Chavin or with those of Tihuanaco, whose extension, even as far as Tierra del Fuego, was far more complex than is generally supposed. It may be that the Polynesians were acquainted with a few survivors of this first race, for there are certainly some traditions that seem to have been handed down.

These Polynesians were marked by a very strong traumatic experience: it was not the effect of chance or of the climate but of the acquisition of an awareness, a knowledge, of such importance that there is nothing comparable to it in the other islands.

It may be that Easter Island will keep its secret: but in our attempt at recasting its history—a history that was the subject of a remarkable analysis by Alfred Métraux—we have opened the way for enquiries into a protohistory or rather a primohistory that appears to have included one of the most tragic phases in man's evolution and in his voluntary migration.

TWENTY

The Great Mystery of the Inscribed Wooden Tablets

The most singular problem is without doubt the existence upon Easter Island of a form of writing that has been called ideographic or pictographic, but whose precise meaning no one has yet been able to decipher.

This writing is all the more extraordinary since up to now no other has ever been discovered in the Polynesian archipelagoes. A great deal of work has been done to decipher these ideographs, since the discovery of the first tablets analysed by Bishop Tepano Jaussen up to the recent labours of Professor Thomas Barthel of the University of Hamburg. None has yet succeeded in providing a real interpretation of the tablets.

Let us examine the problem from the beginning and try to find the exact meaning of what has been called 'the speaking wood'. Here there is a phonetic error, which has falsified the basis of subsequent research. *Kohou Rongo-Rongo* has been translated 'speaking wood'. *Kohou* does in fact mean wood, but the correct pronunciation of the word is *Kohau,* which means inscription: and then again *Rongo-Rongo* means 'transmitting agent'. This gives us a far more literal and more exact meaning. The tablets were 'transmitters of inscriptions or of writing', and the learned men who knew this writing and who taught it were called *Maori Kohau Rongo-Rongo,* which means 'scholar who transmits writing'.

The extreme difficulty of the problem arises from the death of virtually all the Rongo-Rongo scholars in 1862, at the time of the Peruvian raid, and from the rapid collapse of the original culture with the coming of the first missionaries. Mgr Jaussen saw a native who had been initiated by the last of the learned men and he tried to induce him to speak. From the conditions in which the interrogation took place it is reasonable to suppose that the result could not have been particularly valuable; for in the first place only someone unacquainted with the state of mind that is termed primitive and that I call esoteric could expect to obtain any worthwhile revelation all at once and in an atmosphere of examination. Furthermore, it must be recalled that this writing of the initiates may have had three meanings or aspects, like the Egyptian hieroglyphics—esoteric, hieratic, daemonic.

In 1914 Miss Routledge did her best to get into contact with the last of the old men and to persuade them to make certain revelations. She observes that unhappily these last survivors, including one Tomenika to whom we shall refer again later, died a few days afterwards. In any case, and in spite of Miss Routledge's exceptional reliability, I personally do not believe that a native would ever dare reveal a meaning of such a kind to a European, being well aware that the Kohau Rongo-Rongo were holy and not to be handed on to the uninitiated.

In former days the knowledge of this writing was reserved first for the royal family, secondly for the chiefs of the six regions, and thirdly for the Maori Kohau Rongo-Rongo. Because they lost sight of this simple notion of the subject's basically esoteric nature, investigators often obtained curious interpretations, founded upon no more than a dislike of saying no: thus Jaussen, Thomson, Routledge and others assert that they were given differing translations of the same tablet, and that after careful enquiries carried out at intervals of several days.

In 1956 Professor Thomas Barthel worked according to an entirely different methodology. He states that this yielded some results; but what is quite certain is that he did not manage to see a single tablet during his time on Easter Island and that he received no exact information from the natives.

A very interesting work published by M. de Hevesy compares the Easter Island ideographs with those discovered in the excavations at Mohenjo-Daro and Harrapa, on the middle Indus. It certainly seems that this line of enquiry has not been exhausted and that M. de Hevesy's conclusions are of undeniable importance.

We were very much surprised by a strange piece of information that we were given on Easter Island. A native friend told us: 'The first race invented the Rongo-Rongo writing: they wrote it on stone. Of the four parts of the world that were at one time inhabited by the first race, it is only in Asia that this writing still exists.'

Another piece of information recorded by Dr Stephen-Chauvet is that, according to tradition, King Hotu-Matua brought six hundred texts written on banana-leaves with him. This in no way invalidates the first statement, since in any case we do not believe this writing originated on Easter Island.

The great question remains—why does this writing exist only upon Easter Island? Because of the paucity of the research on other Pacific archipelagoes we can give no answer to this.

The one valid contribution that our expedition can bring to the solution of this mystery is perhaps the extraordinary notebook that we have already referred to. When we came to look into it closely, we found that it had in fact belonged to that famous Tomenika of whom Miss Routledge speaks. It appears that he himself drew the ideographs, while their transcription into the old tongue was performed at his dictation by someone else who knew how to write.

This notebook is so important that it calls for months of work, not only to translate the transcription in the old Easter Island language but then, above all, to carry out a classification of the ideographs and to attempt the translation of a tablet.

There is no doubt that this glossary of the ideographs may prove a great help towards the understanding of this form of writing. During the months to come we shall have to work according to two disciplines: in the first place we must try to translate the transcription of the Rongo-Rongo signs into the old language; secondly, we shall have to process the material so that it can be fed into the big IBM computer, which is capable of handling vast numbers of possible solutions, far beyond human powers.

For my part I do not for a moment suppose that the Easter Island writing can be looked upon as a script in the literal sense. We are more of the opinion that the ideographs, like the Quipu or the knotted strings of the Marquesas, stand for an element of thought and thence of speech that is not to be encompassed by our form of transcription. Rather do these characters contain a concentrated power of living expression that is possessed by nothing else except mathematical symbols, which are developing into the sole universal language. Since there are no frontiers that can hinder the transmission and interpretation of Einstein's and Oppenheimer's formulae, the same must certainly have applied to the understanding of the early symbols. To take no more than two examples—all primitive peoples at once recognize and interpret two signs that seem strange to us. First the concentric lines that are to be seen at Carnac and in many other places and that symbolize the waves of life; and then the well-known swastika, whose bent arms began by pointing in the opposite direction to those of the recent notorious example, and which, from Tibet to Easter Island, symbolizes the setting in motion by man of the two unchanging axes of life—axes that, inscribed in a circle, primarily stood for incarnation and sublimation, that is to say, the vital atom; and there is a certain esoteric knowledge that is aware of their dangerous point of intersection.

This book cannot claim to give the answer to the story of the island of giants nor to say the last word about it; what is more, it has two obvious gaps—two results that we cannot yet give. The first is that of the carbon-14 tests carried out on the charred wood that we found in our stratigraphy; and the second is the probable interpretation of the Rongo-Rongo writing, which we cannot undertake in the immediate future, since we are obliged to work independently and without subventions of any kind.

Perhaps one day we may even work in another manner altogether, rejecting the whole of a science that is too often based upon the logic of a world that likes to think itself intelligent but whose actions remain tragically irresponsible.

TWENTY-ONE

Disturbing Facts

There were only a few weeks of living in this island of silence left to us, but there were still a great many words to be written down. As the time for parting approached, the days grew tense and the hours stretched out, so strongly did the islanders feel a renewed zest for life, that is to say, for thought.

We galloped off for one long week, going back to our adventurous discovery of this little world which, with its subterranean and its sublunar aspects, is a double world, double like the intentional shift in perspective of its form of expression. Once more we were to go to the great Rano-Raraku workshop, not only to dwell with the dreaming giants again but also to examine an exceedingly curious architectural phenomenon.

At the top of the volcano's lip, standing more than six hundred feet over the sheer drop, there opens a series of holes and communicating galleries, all cut by human hands. These holes are about three feet across and a little less in depth and they follow one another at regular intervals. Another range of holes, rather lower down, has the gap between the holes pierced by an inner gallery that has been very highly polished by wear.

This combination can be interpreted in many ways. Either the holes were used as look-out posts, or the whole thing may have been a solar observatory. Or it may have served to connect Hotu-Iti and the Rano-Raraku cliff by means of a positive rope-way, as an old man told us it was. This explanation seems to have been made up for the benefit of passing travellers, like the tale of the Poike ditch. Here, as in certain high places, it appears that the true interpretation was of a dual nature, so that secrecy should be preserved.

A friend of ours told us a little more. According to tradition, this arrangement of intercommunicating holes was used as a hoist, a series of winches, which allowed the statues to be manoeuvred on the inner wall of the volcano.

Now a point that had struck us in the very first place was the different and debased style of these figures; on the inner side of the volcano they are of a commonplace technique and what is more of a commonplace stone. So it was possible that as the men of the second migration had lost the mana, they were obliged to invent a logical, mechanical process to move their debased copies of the gigantic statues from the slopes to the foot of the volcano. Taking into consideration the smaller weight of these statues, this theory of a hoisting mechanism seems to be sound. Furthermore, we found lines of wear running down the rock of the inner face of the volcano from the upper complex to the foot of the last place where work was carried out. We give a plan of the whole, hoping that other investigators may work on the problem in time to come.

We also intended to take another look at the question of the famous paved causeways that run into the sea and that have led certain writers to suppose that at one time Easter Island was larger. These causeways are in fact exactly-defined and perfect lava-flows whose surface cracked on coming into contact with the sea. With the passage of centuries these cracks have been worn by the sea-water, so that they give the impression of well-set stones: but the theory does not stand up to the most cursory examination. Nevertheless there do exist three man-made roads on the island and for a few yards they

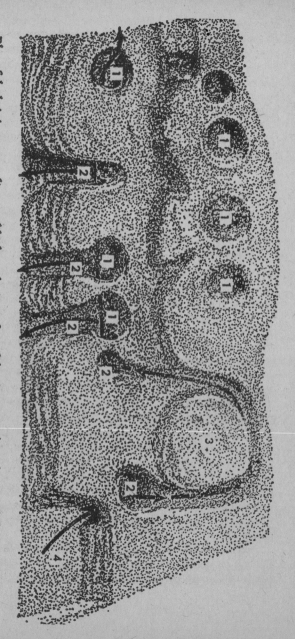

Plan of the hoisting system discovered high on the inner face of the Rano-Raraku volcano: 1 holes to lodge the men who handled the ropes: 2 channels in which the ropes ran: 3 monolith used for snubbing the hoist: 4 cave for storing the ropes

do run into the sea. They are built in very small coves, comparatively sheltered from the surf, and they were certainly used as ports, or more precisely, as runways for boats. Some workers have looked upon them as a proof of communication between the archipelagoes or else as great slides for the embarking of the statues, though from the lie of the land this is far from likely. On the other hand, there is no doubt that these constructions were used by the islanders, their function being ramps for the canoes the natives formerly possessed.

The natural causeways formed by the lava-flows, such as those close to Hangaroa Bay, were certainly made use of, but we were never able to find anything to show that they had been improved or worked upon by men.

We wanted to make a last journey right round the island so as to see all the ahu, all the stone platforms upon which the statues were set up during the second period. One conclusion stands out. All these platforms were built after the second migration, for in all of them there are to be found the slabs used in the construction of canoe-huts—all except the Ahu Vinapu, the one whose style had so impressed me.

There is no doubt about it: the first civilization was destroyed and assimilated by the second migration. But there is one far more remarkable fact—in the three ahu that are traditionally believed to have been built by Hotu-Matua at Anakena there are to be found stones from canoe-huts; and in one of them, forming part of the masonry, there can be seen not only a head whose expression is reminiscent of the kneeling statue of Rano-Raraku but also a very fine basalt carving in a completely different style that shows the flight of two birds.

These are all overlapping aspects of the problem of the peopling of the island, not only by the Polynesians but by those who came before them. I think that in this context the legend of Anua-Motua may not only provide an important contribution but may also put the often-recounted tale of Hotu-Matua (the leader of the last Polynesian migration, no doubt) into its proper perspective.

Every day during those last few weeks my wife went to the leper-house, which the authorities call the sanatorium. There the aged Veriveri was waiting for us; there, for hours on end, we translated his words; and there, in his mud hut, we came to know his wretchedness.

As we see it, the history of the island of silence—I do not say its protohistory—may be summed up thus: it is very likely that in about the fourth century AD men from the Polynesian archipelagoes reached its desolate shores. Then came two successive overlapping migrations, that of Hotu-Matua and that of Anua-Motua. Both reached Easter Island after a long voyage through the Marquesas, Tuamotu and Gambier archipelagoes. All this happened towards the end of the thirteenth century.

On Easter Island these separate migrations found an established culture and also a few survivors of the first race, their powers much diminished. But that first race remains a mystery. It was the Polynesians who built the ahu with statues. It was the first race that left Easter Island its astonishing legacy: this race came from the East and it was not solely what we understand as pre-Columbian. That is the crux of the great problem which must be solved by archeology, for Easter Island is no aesthete's problem: and it remains disturbing.

Here certain traces are apparent of that antediluvian people whose presence we are beginning to discover—a people who will call into question all the temporal and ethical notions that science has tried to force upon us.

As we know of the existence of this antediluvian race and have no doubt that they possessed a superior knowledge of an entirely different world, it seems to me that certain information which we were given on Easter Island and authorized to set down should be communicated in these pages, lucidly, and without hesitation.

When we were in camp we used to have long, anxious conversations by night as we gazed not only at the blazing stars but also at the artificial satellites that often passed overhead. We were told certain things that I here set down in a literal translation, things that seem to me of terrible importance. I write them in the order that I received them.

'The inhabitants of Jupiter have settled the concordance of the planets.

'The statue [taken to Belgium] is one of the oldest, but its virtue has been entirely taken from it.

'The first planet that men will come to know is Venus.

'Our bodies cannot withstand more than two months on the planets.

'All the planets worship the sun.

'Not many stars are inhabited.

'Among us there are people whom we cannot see.

'A very holy tablet was stolen from Easter Island: the city to which it was taken [Louvain] was burnt.

'The current and the light of Venus are produced by the air.

'Two planets, Jupiter and Mars, have no natural electricity: they are like the earth.

'There are no winds.

'Only our earth has men of different colours.

'There is only one sun, and no one can live on it.

'There are people living on the moon.

'There is one planet that has no vegetation and no earth; it is made up of water and rocks alone.

'The sort of human beings who live there are different, and they are born in the water.

'On that planet there are mines of metals unlike ours,

especially one unique metal, finer than gold, whose colour is green-black-blue-yellow-red.

'The planet consists of a ball of rock and iron.

'The iron crust has to be pierced with a fire of stones to get at the metal.

'The fire of stones and water brings the metal out very thin. It can be used as cloth.

'Easter Island was different once.

'There was no rain, but the water welled up from the ground. The island was the same shape: the climate was very hot and huge plants grew on it.

'The island's first race was to be found on two Polynesian islands, in one part of Asia and one part of Africa in which there are live volcanoes.

'An island in the Pacific has been given the dead power of Easter Island to keep.

'On this island—and it is the only place in the world —there still live a few specimens of the ancient tree that used to grow in the four parts of the world.

'The tree of life had no fruit.

'Thousands of years ago the stone of Rano-Raraku was different and hard. It is the change in the climate that has altered the nature of the rock.

'There used to be animals on the island of Matakiterani.

'The volcanoes appeared in the days of the first race.

'First came Rano-Aroi.

'Secondly came Rano-Kao.

'Thirdly came Rano-Raraku: but many years passed between their coming.

'That is all we know.'

So there it is. I know only too well that this document will earn us violent abuse from certain mandarins of science, prudent scepticism from others, the startled perturbation of some readers and perhaps the admiring wonder of others.

This document, which is not ours, should be read over again. For my part I cannot offer any opinion, nor do I wish to do so.

Epilogue

It is all over.

Our boat has returned amid the rain-squalls, and at two tomorrow afternoon we leave. At nine tomorrow the governor will inspect our baggage, alone; but several Chileans and two hundred islanders will watch him. At ten tomorrow my friend Montero will help me bring aboard our assorted baggage. At noon we shall eat the remaining scraps of this meal that has been going on for months. Tomorrow we shall have to tell ourselves impossible things . . . and look as foolish as lovers heartbroken at another's marriage.

And now tomorrow has become today.

With an expressionless face the governor salutes us. The uneasy crowd looks on.

The last boat. Our friends, the friends whose names I have not mentioned in this book, because they have to go on living on the island. The painful hoisting of the anchor. Sorrow. The throbbing of the engine. All hands to the sails!

It is over.

All over.

Ahead of us lie twenty-eight days at sea. Two thousand eight hundred sea-miles to reach that beloved Tahiti, beloved and dying as love dies. But I know that far away, there at the foot of Rano-Raraku, stand the statues whose taut mouths will never speak again and whose eyes watch the stars for ever above Matakiterani, the island at the end of the world.

Calédonien, May 1965
Paris, July and August 1965

Facts about Easter Island

The island lies in latitude 27°8′24″ South and longitude 109°20′ West: it is 2,700 miles from Tahiti and 2,600 from Valparaiso. The Galapagos archipelago lies some 2,000 miles to the north-east. To the south there is the Antarctic. The area of the Island is 45.5 square miles. Its shape is that of a triangle with sides 10, 11 and 15 miles long.

Although it is swept by winds blowing from the Antarctic, the island's climate is temperate. The dry season runs from December to the end of May, and the cold rainy season from June to November.

The island is entirely volcanic and very considerable magnetic variations are observed. It has no harbour and all the anchorages are dangerous.

In 1964 there was only one small beaten-earth airfield, impracticable for long-distance planes. There is a small hospital and a radio-transmitting station.

Bibliography of Works Cited

BARTHEL, THOMAS *Grundlagen zur Entzifferung der Oster-inselschrift.* Abh. aus dem Gebiet der Auslandskunde, Univ. Hamburg, vol 64, Reihe B. Völkerkunde, Kultur-geshichte und Sprachen, Bd 36, Hamburg.

CAILLOT, A. C. E. *Histoire de l'Ile Oparo ou Rapa.* Paris 1932

COOK JAMES *Second Voyage towards the South Pole and round the World, performed in the 'Resolution' and 'Adventure',* 1772–5. London 1777

ENGLERT, SEBASTIAN *Tradiciones de la Isla de Pascua en idioma rapanui y castellano.* Impr. y edit. 'San Francisco', Padre Las Casas, Chile 1939; *La Tierra de Hotu-Matua. Historia, etnologia y lengua de la Isla de Pascua.* Impr. y edit. 'San Francisco', Padre Las Casas, Chile 1948

EYRAUD, EUGENE Lettre au T.P.R. Supérieur générale de la Congrégation des Sacres Coeurs de Jésus et de Marie. Valparaiso, déc. 1864. *Am. Assoc. Propagation de la Foi,* XXXVIII, 52–71, 124–38. Lyon 1866

GONZALEZ Y HAEDO, FELIPE *The voyage of Captain Don Felipe González in the Ship of the Line 'San Lorenzo' with the Frigate 'Santa Rosalia' in company to Easter Island in* 1770–1801, preceded by an *Extract from Mynheer Jacob Roggeveen's Official Log of the Dis-covery of and Visit to Easter Island in* 1772, tran-scribed, translated and edited by Bolton Glanvill Corney for the Hakluyt Society, 2nd ser., vol 13, Cam-bridge 1908

HEVESY, GUILLAUME DE The Easter Island and Indus Valley Scripts. *Anthropos, XXXIII*

HEYERDAHL, THOR *American Indians in the Pacific.* Stockholm 1952; *Aku-Aku: The Secret of Easter Island.* London 1958

JAUSSEN,TEPANO L'Ile de Pâques. Historique et écriture. [Mémoire posthume rédigé par Ildefonso Alazard d'après les notes laissées par le prélat.] *Bull. Géogr. Hist. et Descriptive,* No. 2, 240–70. Paris 1894

LA PEROUSE, JEAN FRANCOIS DE GALAUP, CTE DE *Voyage de La Pérouse autour du monde* (1785–8). Paris, impr. de la République, an. V (1797)

LOTI, PIERRE Expedition der Fregatte 'La Flore' nach der Osterinsel, 1872. *Globus,* XXIII, 5, Braunschweig, 1873; La Isla de Pascua. *Bibl. Géogr. é Hist. Chilena* (de L. J. Silva), Santiago de Chile 1903

METRAUX, ALFRED *Easter Island: A Stone Age Civilization of the Pacific.* London 1957

PINART, ADOLPHE Voyage à l'Ile de Pâques. *Le Tour du Monde,* XXXVI, 225–40, Paris 1878; Exploration de l'Ile de Pâques. *Bull. Soc. Géogr.,* 6. ser., XVI, 193–213. Paris 1878

Reports of the Norwegian Archaeological Expedition to Easter Island and the East Pacific. 2 vols. London 1962

RIVET, PAUL Les Malayo-Polynésiens en Amérique. *Jnl. Soc. Américanistes Paris,* n.s., XVIII, 1926

ROGGEVEEN *see* González

ROUTLEDGE, KATHERINE SCORESBY *The Mystery of Easter Island; the Story of an Expedition.* London 1919; Survey of the Village and Carved Rocks of Orongo, Easter Island, by the Mana Expedition. *Jnl. Roy. Anthropol. Inst., London,* L, 425–51, 1920

STEPHEN-CHAUVET *La Isla de Pascua y sus Misterios.* Santiago de Chile 1946

THOMSON, WILLIAM JUDAH Te Pito te Henua; or Easter Island. *Smithsonian Inst., Annual Report of the Nat. Museum for* 1889, 447–52. Washington 1891

Acknowledgments

The French Easter Island Expedition, under the gracious patronage of Monsieur Maurice Hertzog, of the Fédération Internationale Scientifique de Musée Royale des Sciences Naturelles de Belgique and of the Navy, wishes to thank the companies that shared in its achievements.

Shell, Pechiney, S.E.I.T.A., Olida, Rolleiflex, Paillard-Bolex SOM-Berthiot, Martini, La Spirotechnique, Fosse, Océan, Pernod U.T.A., Terlenka, Plastyvrand, Lustucru, Kodak, Rolex, Toleries de Grenoble, Simmons, Electrolux, Compagnies Assurances Générales, Freitag, Mono, Guigoz, Suchard, Hutchinson, Jet-Gaz Mepps, Tortue, Trigano, Messageries Maritimes, and all who helped us.

JEANE DIXON:

Prophet or Fraud

By Mary Bringle

A chilling analysis of America's most famous and respected seeress.

Jean Dixon is America's number one prophet and one of the most admired women in America. She receives over 2000 fan letters a day. People claimed she predicted—

the assassinations of John Kennedy, Martin Luther King and Robert Kennedy, Marilyn Monroe's suicide and many other events.

Who is this remarkable woman? Is she all her admirers claim? Or is she dangerous and irresponsible?

Here is a searching examination of Jeane Dixon, her personality, her prophecies, her methods, her reputation and her predictions for the future.

JEANE DIXON: Prophet Or Fraud?
by Mary Bringle   T-095-02   95¢

THE TOWER NATURAL HERITAGE SERIES

T-095-9 TIME IS SHORT & THE WATER RISES
by John Walsh with Robert Gannon   95¢
The true-life story of how ten thousand animals were saved from flood in a dense South American rain forest. Recommended by the World Wildlife Fund.

T-095-35 THE GREAT APES by Robert Gray   95¢
A look at the natural life of apes, chimps, gibbons and gorillas, man's closest relatives. Fully illustrated.

T-095-47 THE LEGEND OF GRIZZLY ADAMS
by Richard Dillon   95¢
The biography of a truly individual human being who spent his life in California mountains among the wildlife and counted among his friends the savage animals from whom he got his name.

T-095-50 HARPOON IN MY HAND
by Olaf Ruhen   95¢
A startling look at the customs and life-style of the natives of Tonga who still hunt giant whales from small boats with hand-held harpoons.

T-095-04 THE DIRTY ANIMAL by Henry Still   95¢
A shocking picture of air, land and water pollution that threatens all life on this planet. The culprit, the dirty animal is MAN, and only he can reverse the process. A startling book.

T-095-56 VALLA, THE STORY OF A SEA LION
by Dean Jennings   95¢
A fine, true-adventure story of sea lions and the hazards they face in their desperate battle for survival. Filled with illustrations.

T-095-67 THE LAST OF THE MOUNTAIN MEN
by Harold Peterson   95¢
The true story of a living American legend. Sylvan Hart lives in an isolated Idaho stronghold where he has become a survival expert, artisan and philosopher-historian. The story of a truly outstanding man.

**Tower Publications, Inc., 185 Madison Avenue
New York, N. Y. 10016**

Please send me the books listed below.

ORDER BY BOOK NUMBER ONLY!

Quantity	Book No.	Price
. . . .	. . . .	. . . .
. . . .	. . . .	. . . .
. . . .	. . . .	. . . .
. . . .	. . . .	. . . .
. . . .	. . . .	. . . .
. . . .	. . . .	. . . .
. . . .	. . . .	. . . .
. . . .	. . . .	

I enclose $. . . . .

In the event we are out of stock of any of your choices, please list alternative selections *from the same group* below.

Quantity	Book No.	Price
. . . .	. . . .	. . . .
. . . .	. . . .	. . . .
. . . .	. . . .	. . . .

Name . . . .
(please print)

Address . . . .

City . . . . State . . . . Zip Code . . . . .

(Send check, cash or money order.)
NO STAMPS PLEASE.

Add 15¢ for every Canadian dollar order.
Please allow 2 to 3 weeks for filling orders.
No C.O.D.'s, please.